GROUNDED

ACKNOWLEDGMENTS

Mum, Dad, Vic, Bec and Andy (plus partners and nieces and nephews of course!) for always being loving, interested, involved and encouraging.

Josh and Jack — sorry I keep getting your names mixed up.

The head honchos at The LifeStyle Channel and XYZnetworks for bringing *Moar Gardening* into the world: Bruce Mann, Ric Burns, Sandra Hook, Trevor Eastment, John Reddin and Sonia Andersen. The wonderful Kelly Timms — my right hand woman. The most wonderful people in television — the LifeStyle Channel production team: Louise Oaten, Julie Black, Lorna Marty, Sacha Handsaker, Juanita Moller, Janine Moller, Ben Davies, Penny Fowler-Smith, Andrea dal Bosco, Bev Shroot, Jackie Marhn, Tippi Oberman, Liana Warner, Thekla Orfanos, Sandy Cash, Simon Nummy, Steve Broadhurst, Andy McKean, Grant Loaney, Rhys Loaney, Matt Gormly, Zan Tabart. The LifeStyle Channel publicity team: Sharyn Whitten, Katerina Mavridis and Justine Gray.

The tireless workers: David Wait, Clint Simpson, Simon Dyer, Glen Pickard, Bob O'hea, Mick Hourigan, Pete Brown, Doug Greentree, Simon Altoft and Scott Parker.

All the willing guinea pigs who let me go crazy with their gardens: Megan Brown and Antony Warne, Geoff and Lindy Milne, Scott Lovett and Renae Roberts, Geoff Butler and Michele Mullins, Louise Lammers and Anthony Cahill, and Emma McDonald and sons Ben and Joe McLachlan.

Pia, David, Ruby, Ash and Scott for entrusting me with our new millennium commune garden.

La Rocca Management: Gary La Rocca and Jacky Hewitt.

Kevin Palmer for taking a chance on me way back when.

A very special thank you to Karen McCartney for getting me started in this whole writing game and allowing me the time and space to hone my skills.

Inside Out for allowing us to include chapters of inspiration from other designers.

The designers who allowed me to use their wonderful gardens: Margot Knox and family, Jane Burke, Dieter Schwartz and Rick Day, Susan Munro Ross, Jack Merlo, Carol White, Hugh Main and Jean Waugh.

Michael Wee for your humour and your beautiful photographs.

Thanks to Dulux Paints, Porters Paints, Kennards Hire, Hardware House, Richard Unsworth from Garden Life and Bexley Carringbah Landscape Supplies, Mr Bamboo and Hy-way Sheet Metal.

The lovely Murdoch Books ladies who thought this book would be a good thing to do: Juliet Rogers and Kay Scarlett.

A huge special thank you to Diana Hill of Murdoch Books and Marylouise Brammer (and Freddie) for your unerring support, encouragement, positivity and the pastries and never-ending cups of tea.

Dedicated to Paul and Kelly: thanks for the introducing me to the irreverent Diarmuid Gavin, via videotape sent special delivery from London. It was the inspiration I needed to get adventurous. Paul — you left this earth way too soon.

GROUNDED

DESIGN FUNDAMENTALS FOR GARDENS ANYWHERE

BRENDAN MOAR

PHOTOGRAPHY BY
MICHAEL WEE

MURDOCH BOOKS

CONTENTS

INTRODUCTION

Have you ever wondered what you would miss most if you didn't have a garden? For me it's fairly simple: a place where I could experience the outdoor elements — the sunshine, a cooling breeze, and calming doses of fresh air. Although for me this outdoor connection is at the core of what a garden is all about, I also know that the list of ways gardens can make us feel, what we can do in them, and how they enrich our lives, is endless.

Creating your own garden is your chance to enhance the simple pleasure of connecting with the outside. I personally love to do this by creating a space geared towards making the most of precious spare time, with beautiful spaces for friends and family to loll about in, drinking and eating, soothed by colour and calmed by plants.

So how do you create a garden perfectly suited to you? Though you may have seen a garden in a book or magazine that you think would be your dream garden, I would wager that the garden that truly is perfectly suited to you doesn't exist yet.

This imaginary garden is an original expression of who you are and where you are — it's unique and 100 per cent individual. Discovering what this garden is, though, is perplexing to say the least. The ideas don't just pop into your head out of nowhere. To begin this process of discovery you need to arm yourself with the right tools. The tools in question are not spades and garden trowels; rather, they are thinking tools. And in a nutshell, that's what this book is all about — thinking.

The sort of thinking I'm referring to is not necessarily complex or difficult; it's simply a matter of things to think about when you're out and about taking in the neighbourhood sights, or to bear in mind when you're working up the details of a design for your garden. Primarily it's about seeing things anew: appreciating and analyzing plants and materials in terms of colour and texture; letting go of prejudices towards certain plants or materials based on past experiences; questioning what it is you want from your garden; and understanding why some garden spaces are well used and others are forever deserted. These and a host of other questions, thoughts and ideas make up the first section of the book: the design principles. So do remember that these are principles — not step-by-step 'how to' pointers, but rather the thinking tools to empower you to begin seeing anew, assessing, analyzing, problem solving and creating for yourself.

The second section of the book is devoted to the gardens I designed for The LifeStyle Channel's television series *Moar Gardening*, plus a couple of others you may not have seen. This was a chance to tell the story behind these gardens and how they came into being. Interspersed between each of my garden designs are inspirational gardens designed by people whom I regard as some of the most talented and passionate garden makers and designers I have had the good fortune to meet.

This book doesn't aim to represent the be-all and end-all of everything gardenwise. There is a lot of media devoted to the pursuit of creating and maintaining gardens — this is purely my approach, my take on the subject. My greatest hope is that this book and all it contains stimulates you to think beyond the ordinary and find new and original ways of creating a garden that says something about you and where you are.

Brendan Moar

PART 1 DESIGN PRINCIPLES

A SENSE OF PLACE

Gardens that have a true sense of place have evolved in response to where they are located and who has created them. Jane Burke's garden (above) on the Mornington Peninsula of Victoria, Australia is a delicate balance between finely tuned aesthetics and sound ecological ideals. Margot Knox's mosaic garden (right) in Melbourne, Victoria is a wonderful expression of her artistic talent, a work of art, many years in the making.

KEEPING IT REAL

Gardens come in an infinite number of shapes and sizes, some exude wealth, some spirit, and some are a salute to the everyday. But for me, the ones that I keep getting drawn back to are those that are somehow in touch with where they are, and who's created them. They are true to their creators and they're true to their location — they've somehow managed to pick up on what makes that particular place special and unique, and then captured it in the garden. They've tapped into their sense of place.

It's a theme that I keep coming back to time and again, in life and in this book. The thing is, no matter where we live in the world, we often long for somewhere else — fantasizing that somewhere else is more spacious, better located, greener, lusher, more interesting, warmer, and simply better than wherever you might be. And in this longing for another place we can overlook the rich sources of inspiration that are invariably right under our noses. Instead we'll latch onto some notion of formulated style that comes from somewhere else altogether: Balinese, French, Mediterranean, Moroccan, Italian — you name it, you can pretty much buy it off the shelf. Nine times out of ten these kinds of gardens date in about two nanoseconds.

Quite frankly, the best place for each of these gardens is in their country of origin. Each have reasons for evolving the way they have, and the very reason they are so appealing is that they have evolved a rich sense of place in response to their own natural and cultural influences.

The aim for each and every garden I've designed in this book was to try and practise what I preach (not easy!) and somehow create gardens that say something about where they are and who they're for.

Take inspiration from the gardeners and designers who have done that in their own way in the inspirational garden chapters in this book. Margot Knox (pages 76–9) and Jane Burke (pages 184–7) have both created amazing gardens, both wildly different from each other but

each saying so much about them as individuals and where their gardens are located.

Walking through Jane Burke's garden you are left in no doubt as to where you are, with its combination of sensitive environmental restoration and finely tuned aesthetics; Margot Knox's mosaic garden on the other hand is a place so richly imbued with her own and her family's creative spirit that it's nothing less than spinetingling.

Sense of place refers to that thing, a feeling perhaps, that makes a place special. It's a combination of elements that come together all at once and give you a rich sense of where you are. When you're in a particular place the tricky bit can be putting your finger on what makes that place special. Peculiarly, it's usually when we leave it, when our memory lingers on certain things, that we have a clearer impression of what it was like. Think of, say, a dark rainforest, a pristine high-altitude bushland full of granite boulders and wildflowers, or a windswept coastal heath — you no doubt have an instant sense and appreciation of what it's like to be in those places.

The same goes for the manmade bits as well. Whether it be the backstreets of Harlem in New York, or Circular Quay in Sydney, or your own neighbourhood street — if you closed your eyes and thought back to places of significance to you, I'm sure you could recall a range of visual and other sensory characteristics that make these particular locations tick. Certain places simply have an intrinsic harmony and a certain balance.

In the same way that architecture can create buildings that are in tune with their environments, so too can gardens. The modern beach

house is a sleek stylized homage to contemporary building techniques while employing a palette of materials, shapes and textures that speak of its coastal location. Design that manages to capture and stylize the essence of its location to the point that if you uprooted it and moved it somewhere else it would seem out of place is, for me, a great measure of its success.

At no point do we ever want to lose sight of the vital fact that gardens are for people. This was American landscape architect Thomas Church's catchcry and it's a fundamental, timeless aim. For a garden is the place where we can take the time to live and hopefully be one of the most pleasant, calm and relaxed versions of ourselves that we can ever be.

Each place we visit has its own unique character and personality — sometimes specific elements will remain in our memory, whereas other times it may just be a feeling that the place evoked. The boardwalk and spinifex remind us of the beach, worn timbers and deserted outbuildings reveal layers of history, while vast open spaces can make us feel exposed and vulnerable or perhaps energized and free.

FUNCTION

Deciding what you want to do in the garden is the first step
towards developing a useful and satisfying garden space.
Gardens can be hard-working spaces, maybe used for growing
vegetables and fruit — or more passive places, where all you
want to do is sit and relax.

KICK-STARTING THE DESIGN

Where to begin? Most people I know have some sort of grip on nutting
out how their house is going to come together — the colours they'll
paint it, where the furniture will go, plus a plethora of ideas for future
fantasy renovations. But when it comes to the garden it all goes pear-
shaped. Suddenly there are all these other factors — a garden doesn't
have a roof, for starters — and you're at the mercy of so many more
variables: the weather; this thing called soil — or lack of it; aspect; and
big brown thumbs that turn everything the colour of dead. Then
there's space — sometimes loads of it, sometimes only a skerrick —
and what the hell do you do with it? So it's no wonder many
people just turn on their heels and go back to the safety of the living
room and ponder what colour their new kitchen benchtops are going
to be.

It can be kind of daunting. I find it daunting and I'm meant to
know what I'm doing!

The best thing is to take it in small, easy, bite-sized pieces and do
a lot of thinking before you do any doing. In fact, if you can, a good
rule of thumb is to spend the first twelve months in a new home doing
nothing gardenwise and just living with the space through the full
cycle of seasons. This gives you a chance to truly get a feel for all its
nuances, where the sun and shade fall in winter and summer — where
the sunny spots are in winter and where the shade is over summer —
how cold it gets and probably more importantly just how stinking hot
it can get.

Your very first impressions though are worth hanging on to, as
these are extremely valuable. One of our human strengths slash
weaknesses is our ability to adjust and cope with things that initially
seem impossible to live with. By all means cope and adjust, but take
note of those things that gave you knots in your stomach when you
first moved in. Things like crappy views not only beyond your garden
but also within your garden — the ugly old shed or perhaps the ugly

new shed, for instance. Take note also of the plants, paving, fences: do they add or do they detract? If there are things about the space that seem odd or don't seem to work, try to determine why they don't work: are they the wrong shape, size, colour? Are the spaces in the garden too big, too small, too shady, too exposed, too far from the house? Meditate on it all and ask friends for their honest opinion on what they might do. Become a sponge, soak it all up and see what floats to the surface.

As you are processing all this information, the single most important thing to determine before you start to change, rejuvenate or build a garden from scratch, is what you plan to do in it. It is the modernist's mantra: form follows function. And blow me down, if it doesn't work every single time! You wouldn't build a house without knowing precisely what every room is for, so it really shouldn't be too different in the garden.

The list of things you want to do in your garden doesn't need to be too long or too complicated. As long as you're clear about what it is you want to do out there, then it's a step in the right direction. If you're stuck for ideas on what it is you might do in your garden, pore over books, magazines and the Internet. Not necessarily to find a garden to

The range of activities you want to do in your garden can be the driving force behind how the garden takes shape. A screen (above) doubles as a space divider and an outdoor shower; the lavender rows (right) serve a design function, visually connecting the garden to the broader countryside; a pergola (far right) is in fact a clothesline.

copy (a big no-no as far as I'm concerned), but rather to see what it is that other imaginative folk do in their garden. This sort of research helps enormously, as it's difficult to imagine sunning yourself on the oversized daybed, picking grapes from the sexily designed pergola-come-clothesline overhead, when you're standing staring blankly at a back yard full of nothing.

The range of activities or functions that your garden might provide falls into three categories: active pursuits, passive pursuits and the necessities. The active side of things includes the 'act' of gardening, say, tending a veggie patch or children playing. The passive category refers to the lazier garden activities, such as sitting, lying down and outdoor dining. The necessities are the utilitarian components like the dreaded clothesline, the compost heap, the bins, a shed and maybe a place to park the boat and work on the car if you're so inclined.

This list can then be divided again into the things that are fun to accommodate and include in the garden, and the things (generally the necessities) that are frankly a pain in the neck, as they can seriously upset your aesthetic sensibilities — well, they upset mine at least. The clothesline, the ever-increasing collection of clean-up bins supplied by local authorities and the prefabricated shed being repeat offenders.

These are the things that you can try to screen out and hide, but when space is at a premium (which it is for most of us) it's perhaps wiser to find innovative ways of incorporating them into the design itself. For example, I designed the clotheslines in the suburban gardens of Scott and Renae (pages 96–107) and Jeff and Michele (pages 126–37) to look not like clotheslines but, rather, like pergolas that just

happen to be the right height to hang out a few clothes. Hiding the bins in my own front yard (pages 64–75) was a chance to create a spunky screen that became a character-defining element for the garden.

The list of things that are much more fun to include are the things that are more about living in the garden — places where you can sit, laze around, relax and feast. Not forgetting of course the more active components, namely the growing and tending of plants. Employing the same line of thinking whereby the practical components (such as the clothesline) become design assets rather than liabilities, think about bringing the vegetable patch or herb garden to the fore and making them the star of the show rather than hiding them down in the back corner — as per Emma's veggie garden (pages 112–21).

This, then, is the important list that forms the basis of your design. In the case of Geoff and Lindy's beachside garden (pages 142–51) it was primarily about creating a variety of places to sit, plain and simple. It's a good idea to limit the number of functions so as not to ask too much of a space.

Be cautious also about dedicating vast tracts of your garden to the kids. It's easy to make the mistake that open space equates to play

Think creatively when solving design problems. A sandpit (above) is concealed beneath a garden daybed's removable timber base, while the need to store large rubbish bins becomes an opportunity to create a decorative screen (right). Large sandstone blocks and rendered brick seats (far right) satisfy the need for seating but also complement the earthy palette of materials in the garden.

space. Unless you have half a dozen boys who want to play endless games of football, kids are more comfortable in smaller, more intimate, spaces that are full of interest — lots of plants, spots to hide. The key is more about creating a zone where the kids can get away from the parents. Always remember that kids grow up really fast and that their play needs change as quickly as they grow out of their clothes.

From here you need to flesh out the physical reality involved in carrying out the desired functions in your garden. How many people do I want to seat in the garden? Is it important for the seating arrangements to be flexible? Is shade important? Just how much planting do I want to look after? Am I going to become a zealous green thumb or will I be realistic about my horticultural inadequacies?

Once you're clear about the details of what you want to do in the garden, you're ready to think about arranging or re-jigging the spaces and thinking about the flavour, the mood, and the feel of the garden — and how it expresses something about you and quite possibly where you are.

However, before taking this next step, make sure you do one little thing — draw up an accurate base plan of your garden showing all the built elements and the major planting beds, plants and trees. Keep a clean original and make scribbles and sketches to your heart's content over the top on tracing paper — might sound all a bit professional, but you'll find it's a lot easier to move the barbecue spot around on paper a hundred times until you're happy with it than doing it in 3D reality!

BOUNDARIES

A garden with blurred boundaries — the timber deck appears to
float in space while the view from this garden into the eucalypt
forest is accentuated and exaggerated by the silver frame.

DEFINING SPACE

Every garden has boundaries, some of them visible, some of them not.
They can block out the world and cocoon you, or act as a subtle,
sometimes invisible, transition between you and all that surrounds
you. Then there are the boundaries within your garden that break up
and play with space, making it appear larger or perhaps more intimate.
But just like the walls, windows and doors in your house, your garden
boundaries are the most fundamental components in defining space
and setting the tone for your garden.

In smaller garden areas like courtyards (and even in an average
suburban block) they become the backdrop to the entire space,
considerably influencing the mood and the feel. In larger gardens the
outer boundaries are generally more invisible, becoming less apparent
the further they are from the main outdoor living area of the garden.
As a result, the boundaries within the garden, such as planting beds
and freestanding screens and walls, become more important —
breaking up the space and giving it a more human, manageable scale.

The external boundaries of these gardens can often be their greatest
asset or their biggest drawback. And whatever state they're in will
determine how much work you have to put into either covering them
up in an effort to improve them or allowing them to be an integral,
featured part of the garden.

A lot of people put an enormous amount of energy into trying to
grow things that will conceal dodgy boundary fences, when putting
that same energy into the boundary itself can make it worthy of
showing off, taking the emphasis off the success or the failure of
your planting.

Boundaries can, however, be the most problematic element in your
garden. Ninety-five per cent of the time you're stuck with them, and
the prospect of changing them is a headache in terms of cost or
negotiating with neighbours who may not share your conviction that
you should do something about them. Different councils or local

authorities will have different by-laws that affect boundaries, but in general the cost of building boundary fences or walls is meant to be shared by you and your neighbour 50/50. This is where your powers of diplomacy and negotiation come into play — if you want something a little spiffier than a regular paling fence and your neighbour doesn't, you will probably have to pay the extra yourself if your neighbour agrees to the spiffy option but doesn't want to fork out the extra cash.

If you are building from scratch, it's often best to keep things simple in terms of the boundaries. There are all sorts of variations on the humble timber paling fence, but I must admit the one that I keep coming back to for simplicity and charm is the regular hardwood paling fence. More often these days timber fences are made of treated pine to combat irritating (and destructive) termites. Not as lovely, in my opinion, as the weathered silver patina of a hardwood fence, but nevertheless functional and termite-resistant.

The existing fence in Scott and Renae's suburban garden (pages 96–107) was a prime example of a hardwood paling fence that was termite-free and in good order. There was no need to get into a lather about screening it with planting, because it was worthy of bringing into the design to help reinforce the tone and mood — essentially

Boundaries set the tone and feel of a garden, but they needn't be overly complicated or expensive. The humble hardwood paling fence (above) is a simple, elegant boundary often dismissed as plain and uninteresting. The slate wall (right) and coloured masonry walls (far right) mask ugly sheds, vastly improving the garden's internal views and creating essential backdrops to the spaces.

Australian, unpretentious and simple. It then became a backdrop for a selection of grasses such as miscanthus and pennisetum.

On the über-practical side of things, there are the prefabricated solid sheet metal fences. The most I can say about these fences, without appearing rude, is that they're solid, practical and economical — and that's all!

The problem with boundaries is that you are invariably stuck with a mish mash of fence and wall types in various states of disrepair, plus unsightly views not only beyond your own garden space but also within your garden space. An open-sided carport or aesthetically challenged shed can totally undermine any good work you do in other parts of your garden. Both Megan and Ant's inner city garden (pages 156–67) and Michele and Jeff's reinvented suburban garden (pages 126–37) suffered from this common dilemma. The solution in both cases was to conceal these poor views and undesirable elements with either freestanding walls or walls that boxed in the problem structure. These walls then became invaluable backdrops to the garden spaces.

To combat the mish mash of boundary types it's a case of assessing the best components of your boundaries, and then maintaining those and dealing with the rest. For Megan and Ant, beyond the carport and shed dilemma, there were two opposing types of paling fences on opposite sides of the space — one in good order and running level, the other of the lapped and capped variety and a bit all over the shop in terms of level and alignment. The solution was to keep one (the good one of course) and mask the other one. Masking meant simplifying it and making it look for all intents and purposes like a rendered

masonry wall. Rendered masonry walls (or fake rendered masonry walls in Megan and Ant's case) are terrific boundary solutions. They're clean, simple and solid, and are a blank slate for colour and texture to be applied if you so choose — eventually serving as excellent backdrops for planting and other elements such as sculpture.

Beyond the paling fence and rendered masonry walls there are of course a myriad solutions for boundaries: stone walls, natural reed cladding, and many variations of steel and timber. Not forgetting too that there are also means for 'faking' these finishes. Jeff and Michele's reinvented suburban garden was a good example of a site where all of these approaches and solutions for boundaries came into play. The combination of a pretty horrible mass-produced sheet metal fence and 'lollipopped' conifers was a serious handicap for the garden. A combination of solutions created a mix of boundary types that worked together as a harmonious palette. The metal fence was either clad directly with fibre cement sheeting or a freestanding wall was built in front of it. The fibre cement sheeting faked the look of a masonry wall and became a good example of the range of solutions you can apply to these walls. One wall was painted with a totally matt dirty red and the other with a rust paint effect. Complementary and contrasting texture

A timber screen (above) creates a much-needed vertical element and relates to a similar screen at the property boundary. Open screens maintain a sense of spatial flow and double as decorative features and safety barriers (top right), and backdrops and wind breaks (right). Paving and decking patterns on the garden floor (far right) can also delineate different spaces within the garden.

and warmth were then introduced via strips of reed cladding, breaking up the rust walls. The freestanding concrete block wall masking the shed was clad with fake stacked slate (genuine slate, but only slivers of slate, glued together as tiles).

With the built boundaries in good order you are freed somewhat in relation to planting: rather than just choosing plants to do the hard work of concealing and masking, you can choose plants for a wider range of reasons — reasons of aesthetics and mood and space enhancement. For example, the bamboo used in Megan and Ant's garden helps to really foster that green, cool, tropical feel Megan was after. With the walls behind them acting as plain backdrops of colour, the bamboo is shown off to maximum effect, enabling you to fully appreciate its form, colour and foliage.

In larger gardens, beyond the average suburban block, boundaries become more about defining space within the garden. Starting a large garden from scratch can be a daunting task as you try to work out what to do with all that space. It becomes a case of breaking space down into smaller spaces — not all of the same size, as that makes them dull and uninteresting to explore, but into a variety of spaces, some intimate, some vast. Even in the smallest of gardens it's possible to break up the space. In limited spaces this has the effect of making a small area seem larger, as you can't see it all in one go. In both large and small gardens, dividing space works best when there is a reason for doing it: breaking spaces up according to their different functions is a good start.

Rather than using solid walls or screens to divide space within a garden, I find that semi-transparent boundaries seem to maintain a better flow of space through a garden. Freestanding timber or steel climbing plant supports — slatted timber similar to that in Geoff and Lindy's beachside garden (pages 142–51) or the steel reinforcement mesh at the large country garden 'Campton' (pages 80–91) — have a lightness to them and somehow suggest that the space keeps flowing through them rather than being totally contained as would be the case with solid masonry walls.

Naturally, planting beds are the simplest way of dividing up space within a garden — hedges are a very structured way of achieving this, but consider softer options too such as the row of miscanthus in the beachside garden (pages 142–51). Without pretending to be a full-blown screen, the row of grass simply takes the edge off the view of the car that is housed in the adjacent driveway.

Space can also be effectively divided at ground level. The patterns different garden floor materials make are just as successful in delineating different zones and spaces as vertical boundaries. The different treatments of gravel, paving and decking in both Jeff and Michele's reinvented suburban garden (pages 126–37) and Emma's vegetable patch (pages 112–21) effectively divide the space without relying on vertical elements. In these gardens the spaces flow into one another, similar to an open plan living room. The feeling of spaciousness is maintained, and in fact enhanced: separate zones, each catering for a different activity, create the impression that with so many goings-on the space must be bigger than it is.

CHOREOGRAPHY AND
CONNECTIONS

The transition point between inside and outside is one of the most important in your garden. Keeping the garden easily accessible from the house via windows and openings will help to ensure your garden is used as much as possible. The garden space closest to the back door is an ideal place to create an outdoor dining or tea and chat spot.

MAKING THE MOST OF SPACE

I'm a firm believer that gardens are first and foremost about people — gardens are there to be enjoyed, to be lived in, and inhabited. I find it quite staggering how often I come across gardens that seem to have everything going for them, except that for some reason they're rarely used and in certain cases *never* used. With garden space being the first casualty of denser housing developments and inner city rejuvenation, it's almost criminal to see good garden space go to waste.

Counteracting space waste more often than not comes down to how well connected you are, and whether or not you've got your choreography under control.

Choreography and connections in the garden are all about how people move into and around a garden space. Connections include those transition points between house and garden and from area to area within the garden itself. The overall aim is to make the connections as fluid as possible so that movement in and around the garden occurs on a subconscious, subliminal level. If you have to make an effort to use a space, chances are you won't use it. Being the lazy creatures that we humans are, we need it all to be simple and easy to navigate — for a space to be used effectively, our passage through it should happen in an unconscious, natural way, no thought required.

The choreography analogy is all about control. It's essentially a manipulative thing, making people move through a garden in the way that you want them to — politely forcing them to walk in a certain direction, enticing them from one space into another using devices such as paths, space-dividing elements and focal points. The end result being that your garden is brought to life by people using and exploring every part and aspect of it.

The most crucial connection to begin with in my book is the one between house and garden. You can have the most beautiful, toiled-over garden in the whole world, but if you can't see it clearly from the house, the motivation to get out into it is greatly reduced — the kitchen and living room are usually the heart of the home and generally your biggest competition in getting people to move beyond the back door. Establishing seamless indoor/outdoor flow is something most of us are up to speed on these days, and opening up the back of a home to connect house and garden has to be one of the most popular renovations. If you can afford it, go for it. I'm all for a nice set of bifolds or concertina windows that fold away to give you unfettered access between out and in.

For people who go down this route, it's invariably a life-changing experience — suddenly they live in both house and garden in a way they hadn't quite anticipated. If you aren't ready to spend the many thousands of dollars this sort of renovation can swallow up, think about putting in a more modest, strategically placed window that gives you a view into the garden — if you can at least see the garden, there's every chance you'll want to get in amongst it.

Once you're past the back door, there are a host of other connections to take into consideration, beginning with that area right outside the back door. This has the potential to become the most actively (or passively!) used part of the garden, by virtue of its location hard up against the house — particularly if the interior living area of the house is adjacent. A covered verandah, timber deck or paved space can become the key outdoor living area and the most logical spot to think about locating an outdoor dining or nice simple tea and chat spot. If you are considering a deck or paved area, make them big enough to accommodate the furniture you have in mind plus space to move the chairs in and out easily: an area about 3.5 x 3.5 metres (11½ x 11½ feet) is a safe guide as a minimum.

Too often, however, people get stuck at this outdoor dining/living zone and don't venture further into the garden. This could be because there is a physical barrier in the form of a railing, a badly located set of steps off the verandah or deck or too great a level change, or quite simply because there is no good reason to explore any further — the prospect beyond being altogether uninspiring.

In terms of level change being a hindrance to further exploration, it doesn't take much of a level change to discourage people from moving off the deck or patio into the rest of a garden space. Three or four steps is about the max before your auto lazy instinct clicks in and you think 'Naaaah, I'll just stay here — I'd just have to walk back up the steps anyway!' It might sound dubious, but test this little theory out next time you're at a friend's place with multiple steps off the rear deck or patio and I swear you'll see my point.

Level change is where you can introduce some of that sneaky manipulative movement management. Regular steps can be a bit of a turn-off for lazy garden punters. Instead I'm a big fan of broad,

Getting people off the deck and down into the garden is often one of the biggest design challenges. Generous, wide platforms that don't look like regular sets of steps can often coax people down a level change that they may otherwise find off-putting.

generous steps and platforms that make something of the level change, and which are a much subtler method of encouraging people to traverse a change in ground level — before they know it they've made the trek and they're down (or up) in the guts of the garden.

But to pull them up or down those platforms — or if you're dealing with a more or less level space, out into the garden — you've got to have something worth going to, some sort of magnet. This generally comes down to one of two things:

1 Another space with a defined function such as a barbecue area, a pool perhaps, a vegetable patch or an irresistible sunny (or shaded) place to relax; or,

2 A focal point or something of interest — a view, an artwork or sculpture, a planting or even a simple seat.

Endowing another space with an important function beyond the main outdoor living space adjacent to the rear of the house is a very effective option to get people moving around and through your garden. I like to think of these spaces as being like the milk fridge in a supermarket. Ever noticed how the essentials in supermarkets are located in the furthest corner so that you have to walk through the entire store? The thinly disguised ulterior motive being to encourage you to spend up on things you spy along the way. This was the exact thinking behind the clothesline/pergola combo in Renae and Scott's suburban garden (pages 96–107).

Focal points can be just as powerful a device to pull people through spaces — in fact, gardens without them can be pretty bland affairs. Focal points are areas or, more literally, points of focus, that

your eye can lock onto. They help us to navigate the space visually and physically. In a small garden or courtyard, focal points in the form of feature plants, pots or sculpture punctuate the space and create much-needed interest. A bit of the old less is more philosophy comes into play here — too many focal points and their visual pulling power is lost and things just start to look cluttered. That's not to say you can't have more than one focal point, it's more a case of a hierarchy of focus. It's best to let one object or plant dominate, then allow a series of others to gently animate other parts of the garden. This is a way of controlling and building the drama within your garden.

In larger gardens, focal points are critical in helping to move you physically through a garden. In formally laid out designs of avenues and straight lines, focal points need to be employed, otherwise the axes that are set up will be for nothing — missing their expected climax. In a more organic, freeform space, focal points assist in making sense of it all. Placing a feature (which can also be a view or an opening into another space) at the end of each change of direction will help to pull people around and through the spaces.

Again, in larger gardens movement from space to space naturally occurs when one space is a marked contrast to its neighbouring space. The simplest contrast is size. If you have two spaces the same size next to each other there is no great impulse to move from one to the other — it's all a bit dullsville and sameish. With the neighbouring space being twice as big or half the size, the scale and mood are altered, creating a more dynamic spatial relationship and compelling the visitor to investigate the 'different' adjacent space.

Perhaps the most obvious way to direct people around your garden is via a combination of defined paths and obstacles. But back to that lazy theme — we're slaves to our desires, or more accurately, desire lines. The path of least resistance is something all humans succumb to in the garden, showing little regard for marked-out paths or even barriers. We'll veer from the path and go through or over the top of barriers if it means we don't have to walk as far. This is where the choreography around a garden is a fine balance between you deciding where you'd like people to walk and the path that people naturally want to take. The main desire lines will generally run between access points such as doorways and gates and between key function zones. It doesn't mean that paths have to be literally straight lines between these points, but you should use these lines as a very solid starting point and basis for where the paths will run.

Blockages or obstacles (as I refer to them) can be things like planting beds, low walls, built-in seats or hedges and screens — they help greatly in directing traffic in the third dimension, as opposed to paths which only do it on the ground plane. The denser or more

substantial the blockage, the less likely we will be to ignore it and the more we will respect the route the path is indicating.

One of the best times to see how people use your garden and to get a feel for where people naturally gravitate — and how they get there — is when you're having a gathering of people who don't normally live with you. Take note of the desire lines, the shortcuts people are taking and where they're sitting. It's a good time to consider making adjustments in order to get the most out of your space, and if everyone is sticking to the kitchen you know that you've got a lot of work ahead of you!

Focal points, paths and obstacles are tools to help draw people through the garden, making them go where you want them to. The lavender rows (bottom left) direct people's movement while the barbed wire ball beckons for closer inspection. The tree trunk and the positioning of the sandstone block (top left) ensure people stick to the path and are not tempted to take a shorter route though the garden bed. The steel ball (above) creates a dramatic focal point.

SCALE, BALANCE AND PROPORTION

To improve the intimacy of this verandah space, certain elements had to be adjusted — it was a matter of getting the scale right. Its high ceiling needed to be lowered to make the space feel more intimate and less exposed. The issue was solved by suspending bamboo blinds (out of shot) from the 'ceiling' and hanging metal planters (top right corner), which shielded the space to a degree. The decking at ground level and the plants are also integral in creating an intimate environment.

DESIGN'S BUILDING BLOCKS

Designing gardens is primarily about the manipulation of space. That space is made up of a myriad elements conceived in both two and three dimensions. The elements are the plants, boundaries, structures, furniture and the garden floor. In conceiving and designing the space and the elements that comprise it, there are some handy, somewhat esoteric, concepts to get your head around: scale, balance and proportion. Master these I say and the design world is your oyster!

At the root of it all is a thing called human scale — it's how we read space and the things around us, making sense of it all in relation to our own human proportions. Reading and evaluating scale is something we're doing constantly without being consciously aware of it. It can have a range of effects on us, from making us feel vulnerable and intimidated, to making us feel safe and protected. Compare the vibe in the cathedral-like proportions of an almighty multinational's entrance foyer with that of a cosy backstreet café. One is all power, might and intimidation; the other is welcoming, warm and relaxed.

For me there are two ways of looking at scale in the garden: getting the scale 'right', and playing with scale for effect. Getting the scale right is about achieving a sense of balance and correct proportion between the size of elements within a garden, and the overall size of the space. The best interior analogy would be large overstuffed couches in the living space of a small apartment — too bulky and crowded.

The outdoor room concept is now part of everyday garden renovation speak. More than anything its greatest merit is encouraging the creation of spaces with scale and proportions similar to those inside our homes. We are naturally comfortable in spaces of this scale — they are spaces that we will truly live in, as opposed to a large open grass area that we rarely venture into unless armed with a lawnmower or a cricket bat.

Getting the scale right is also about creating spaces within a garden that are conducive to favourite human pastimes like chatting and

interacting. Again a simple analogy is the lounge room. Two couches facing each other at just the right distance apart encourage conversation — as opposed to couches set right back, barn-dance style, around the perimeter of a room. This concept is one to keep firmly in the front of your mind when considering the size of paved spaces, the alignment of retaining walls that double as sitting walls, and the location of built-in seating.

Playing with scale for effect gets us into the realm of optical illusion. Here we take the rules and ideas regarding getting the scale right and play around with them. There is a concept known as overscaling — whereby a large object is placed in a small space where you wouldn't naturally expect it to fit. A large oversized urn, say about 2 metres (6¹/₂ feet) tall, placed in a small courtyard will create serious impact, but it will also psychologically suggest the courtyard space is bigger than it really is. This concept also works with pavers on the garden floor. Pavers that are larger than 300 x 300 millimetres (about 1 x 1 foot) will help to visually enlarge the size of a relatively small space because of their clean, uncomplicated lines as opposed to regular brick-sized paving, which can be overly patterned, visually shrinking a space.

Large pavers help to reduce the visual clutter characteristic of smaller pavers, making a space appear larger (above). Play with asymmetry and place pots and sculptures (right) of varying sizes around the garden for more dynamic results than the predictability of formal symmetry. Pergolas and other garden structures should be designed simply so as not to overwhelm and dominate the house (far right).

When placing sculpture or pots in a space it's better, I find, to err on the side of generosity — small pots or small bits of sculpture can easily get lost even in the smallest of spaces.

The successful design and inclusion of three-dimensional components in the garden, be they walls, pergolas or arbours, depends largely on getting their scale and proportions right as well as balancing them with all other components in the garden — especially the house. When I first developed my garden design obsession I read and re-read a book on Australia's original garden guru, Edna Walling. In it she had some theories about the proportions of garden structures, and I think they were some of the wisest words ever written. Her basic idea was to keep freestanding pergolas and arbours low and broad — too high and they become gangly and unsteady looking. Similarly, Edna was a fan of generously sized timbers — particularly when used for the posts; this keeps them looking solid, earthed and grounded.

Balancing these structures with the house is just as important a consideration, and one safe rule is to make sure the house is always the dominant-looking structure scalewise. The pergola in Jeff and Michele's reinvented suburban garden (pages 126–37), for example, is a bold simple structure, but its proportions, orientation and location ensure that it doesn't compete with the house.

Balance is something to be considered throughout the design process, from the broad overall layout to the detail of locating pots. It is often mistaken for symmetry — objects of equal size and shape located equidistant from a central axis. This is certainly one type of balance, but asymmetry is also a form of balance. Asymmetry balances

large and small objects in the same composition or space with no apparent axes.

Symmetry is the tool of the formal classical approach to design — think Versailles. Symmetry represents order, logic and control. In applications on a mega scale like Versailles, it symbolizes humankind's dominion over nature. Asymmetry on the other hand is almost the reverse — it's wilder, less predictable, more organic and in my opinion a much more exciting design tool.

My own preference is to use both symmetry and asymmetry in the one design. Employing symmetry and central axes is something that is very useful when linking a garden design to the house. Axes projected out from elements such as doorways and the central alignment of a building are useful for establishing a logic and framework up close to the house. As you move further out into the garden, the more organic nature of asymmetry can help to loosen up a design, making it more dynamic and more likely to blend with a natural landscape.

Michele and Jeff's garden is a good example of asymmetry taking over further out into the garden, distant from the house. The 10 metre (33 feet) long snake seat and the circular water feature are two totally

different shapes, but one helps to balance the other. If the water feature was absent, for example, the design would seem lopsided — the snake seat would overbalance the garden. The snake seat needs something to balance it — but not another snake seat.

Similarly, in the placing of pots, two matching containers either side of a doorway or entranceway can help to define an entry and set a formal tone to a space — but care should be taken as this can easily tilt into the realm of twee and kitsch. Instead I prefer to play around with large and small pots balancing one another. Treating pots in this way means they can work as freestanding groups, whereas symmetrically arranged pots need to relate to something architectural or to an entrance, otherwise they'll look out of place — like a fish out of water.

The trick in getting asymmetry working is to use an obvious contrast in the size of elements — for instance, the snake seat and the mosaic water feature in Jeff and Michele's garden. As another example, if you were to place a large sphere on the ground — say, 60 centimetres (2 feet) in diameter — then for effective asymmetrical balance you would need another sphere nearby of at least a third its size — say 20 centimetres (8 inches) in diameter. The smaller sphere placed adjacent to the larger sphere would have the effect of grounding the larger sphere and making it feel like it's meant to be there. The large sphere on its own could look a little lonely.

By taking on these ideas of scale, balance and proportion, you can start to see how they're incorporated into architecture, furniture design, and even the way our streets are laid out on a citywide scale. Start to analyze why you feel comfortable in some spaces and a little edgy in others, and invariably you'll discover that these three design principles play a big role. Once you develop an appreciation for them, you can start to manipulate and control them to your benefit in your own garden.

Pots of matching form and shape but contrasting size make for an interesting asymmetrical composition (far left). The circular fountain and surrounding 'doughnut' of clipped buxus counterbalance the bold serpentine curve of the cement-rendered seat (left).

PLANTING

Variegated foliage such as the leaves of *Miscanthus sinensis* 'Variegatus' (far left) is useful as a contrast against dark-coloured walls or plain green-foliaged plants. White English lavender (*Lavandula angustifolia* 'Alba') and purple larkspurs (*Consolida* sp.) combine to create a classic, peaceful colour combination.

LET THERE BE LIFE

I never fail to be blown away by the transformation that takes place when a bare garden, with all the hard bits done — the paving, the fences, the walls and the structures — is filled with plants. Of course I'm talking about gardens that are constructed from whoa to go in a matter of weeks, but plants growing and doing their thing in any garden over time without doubt represent the most satisfying and wondrous part of garden making.

It can also be the most perplexing. Whether you're taking on an established garden or starting from scratch, those planting beds either full or bare can be daunting, to say the least. It's a case of ascertaining your horticultural aptitude — some people take to it like a duck to water, while some just can't shake their pathological plant killer ways.

Whatever your skill level, there are some logical ways into the planty end of garden making — some of them are about common sense while some of them are about unburdening yourself from past horticultural baggage and seeing things anew.

As with any other part of the garden design process we want to go straight to the end result — we see a luscious photo of a garden in a magazine and want ours to be exactly like it. Although this can be helpful in terms of inspiration, it's often really just leaping ahead without considering the specific things affecting your garden and its as yet unthought-of possibilities. Plantwise, this means being determined to plant delphiniums because they're your favourite flower which you've been desperate to try out for years, when in reality they're entirely unsuitable; and similarly, holding a complete aversion to succulents because your evil mother-in-law grew them when in fact they could be the perfect solution to your H_2O woes.

Get counselling if required, but do whatever you need to do to get past these hang-ups and move on! Your gardening life will be much easier if you're able to choose plants for all the right reasons — appropriate to your particular site and doing the jobs you need them

to do. A helpful thing to start doing is looking at plants in terms of their inherent visual and design characteristics. Walking down the street you'll start to notice that those dietes growing in the road's median strip have great vertical, strappy form, a lovely dark grey-green matt leaf and a mighty stunning white and purple iris-like flower.

And walking down the street and around the block is the best way to get a feel for what grows in your area. Particularly what grows in the more unkempt, seemingly unloved gardens — whatever is thriving here is almost guaranteed to do the same in your garden.

By all means visit your local nursery and find out what they sell. In most cases nurseries will stock plants that are suited to your area, but for the more unusual plants that also thrive in your area seek out any specialist plant nurseries that might be close by. These are often staffed by people who dedicate their entire lives to the pursuit of finding and growing the more uncommon plants appropriate for your area.

But it's time to take a breath — we're getting ahead of ourselves. Before you open your wallet it's best to have some type of plan.

A good method of selecting plants and breaking free of any emotional botanical shackles is to think of plants as just another element, as building blocks. They just happen to be the building

The sculptural trunks of crepe myrtle (*Lagerstroemia indica*) and fine vertical foliage of the rush *Juncus effusus* (above) are highlighted against a deep red wall. Bold simple rows (right) of *Lavandula* x *intermedia* and artemisia create a graphic planting scheme. *Canna* 'Tropicana' (far right) with its striped foliage injects long-lasting colour into a scheme, as opposed to more fleeting flowers.

blocks that bring the garden to life. It's all getting back to the function thing. Before you get swept away by purist colour schemes or the promise of bountiful blooms, think what jobs you need the plants to perform for you. Do you need plants to screen you from the neighbours? Plants to define spaces within the garden? Do you want them to give you shade?

Whenever I approach a scheme I try to break the plants and their tasks into the following categories: (1) trees, (2) space definers, (3) fillers, (4) structural plants, and (5) showy plants.

I consider trees the heroes of the garden. They can do all sorts of jobs from screening to shading, having a sculptural presence in their own right and creating wonderful unique spaces under their canopies.

The space definers are the hedging and screening plants. They can mask unsightly views, create privacy and divide up space within the garden. They can be clipable formal hedges, looser billowing shrubs or something tall and narrow. They're generally plants that have the capability of growing taller than 1.5 metres (5 feet).

Fillers do exactly that, fill up space. Shrubs and grasses do this very well and are the things to use en masse to provide bulk in a planting scheme and to build up a 'backdrop' against which other plants are contrasted.

Structural plants are the ones with strong form that give focus to a scheme when everything else is becoming a little too soft and fluffy.

The showy plants are the ones that add sizzle to a scheme. Flowers, coloured foliage, the works. These plants should be stealing the show. They're also the ones that you should be prepared to shift and change

to keep things interesting. For that reason, these plants often work well in pots so they can be moved into view when they're doing their thing.

Naturally this is a only a rough guide, but it's an approach that can help enormously both in determining the functions you require your plants to satisfy and in broadly 'blocking out' a planting scheme in three dimensions.

The next step involves fundamental considerations that have a huge bearing on what you will and won't be able to plant: climate type, soil, sun and shade, and moisture.

It's nothing to get nervous about, but you should have a basic understanding of how these factors affect your particular garden — armed with this knowledge, you and your local nurseryperson can start speaking the same language, and you can devour those plant books with an informed mind.

Climate type is something you're stuck with, and in Australia ranges from hot, humid tropical to cool temperate and everything in between. Of particular concern is how cold your winters get and how hot your summers get. If your garden is affected by winter frosts this will limit your ability to grow a huge range of frost-tender plants; hot humid summers will preclude growing heat-sensitive plants. Your proximity to the coast and your height above sea level add another round of factors, such as salt-laden winds on the coast, which will severely limit what you can and can't grow. In all these considerations your local nurseryperson is your best friend and an invaluable source of information.

Soil is something you do have the power to change. As dull a subject as it may seem, without gaining an understanding of your soil type you may as well hang up your trowel now. Soil science is of course a huge subject, but the key is working out how well drained your soil is and how fertile it is. Soil type can be broken into three broad categories: sandy soil, loam and clay soils. Sandy soils are easy to dig and are well drained but don't retain a lot of moisture or goodies for your plants to feed on. Clay soils are the virtual opposite: they are hard to dig and become rock hard when it's dry, but quickly turn to a quagmire when it's wet as they are so poorly drained. They are, however, pretty rich in nutrients. Loam is the prized soil, falling somewhere in between clay and sandy soils: relatively easy to dig and well drained but also retaining moisture and plenty of nutrients.

If you are in doubt about your soil type, take a half-bucket to your nursery and they'll be able to help you out. If you want to get really clever, buy a soil-testing kit to determine your soil's pH levels. It is useful to see if your soils are excessively acid or alkaline, as some plants have either an aversion to or a preference for either extreme.

Providing your soil doesn't just comprise building rubble and buried softdrink cans, your soil type needn't be a huge worry if you stick to plants that are indigenous and already growing in your immediate area. Jane Burke's restored bushland garden (pages 184–7) is an almost perfect example of this approach. However, for many people — particularly in urban situations — this isn't an option, and they need to improve their soil in some way. Speaking very generally,

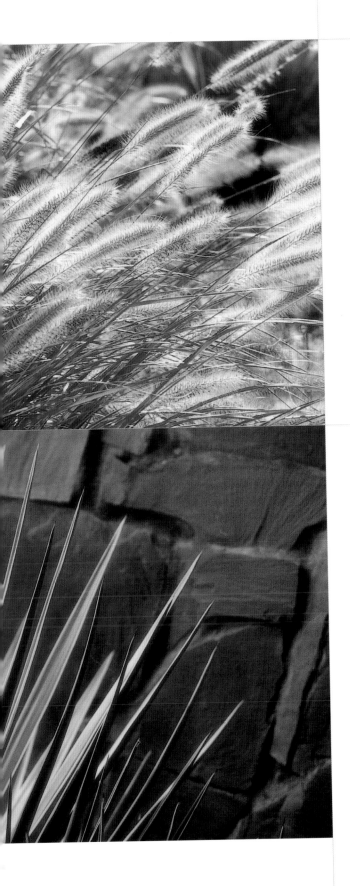

the answer to many woes including low fertility, poor drainage and excessive drainage is to add lots of organic matter in the form of well-decomposed compost and manures — the more the better. Don't skimp on this. If you only add a pitiful spadeful per square metre (10 feet or so), it's not going to do much — spread it on thick and fast and dig it in well. Learn to love the act of digging — your hard work will be rewarded with happy, healthy plants.

Sun and shade are purely about observing rather than giving your back a work-out. There are sun lovers and shade lovers and there are some that are bi-aspectal (a new word I just created). Be clear on how many hours of sun and shade an area receives and at what time of the year — this is going to be more of that valuable information that will help the nurseryperson help you. This is important: don't be vague on this one — take the time to learn your sun/shade stats.

As far as water goes, where Australia — and increasingly many other parts of the world — is concerned, you could safely generalize and assume that moisture, either from the sky or from the tap, is always going to be in short supply. It's crunch time in this regard, and time to think about the most efficient methods of watering and managing moisture loss. The most responsible approach is to choose

Pennisetum (top left), like all grasses, takes on an incredible glow when backlit by the sun — grasses are also great 'filler' plants. The sword-like leaves of this yucca (left) create a strong focus in a planting scheme and offer great structural contrast to softer planting. Coloured foliage plants like *Phormium* 'Maori Magic' (above) can work equally well planted in pots which can be moved around the garden where and when you need highlights of colour.

the more drought-tolerant plants — which are extremely well marked at nurseries these days — combined with frequent generous mulching.

Frankly these are exciting times in garden design. Water shortage is often taken as a negative — which it most certainly is; however, through adversity comes change and, hopefully, good things. The good things will come in the form of new, artfully designed waterwise gardens employing tough but spunky plants, the overall result being infinitely more in tune with an Australian aesthetic and sense of place. Again, Jane Burke's garden (pages 184–7) and Hugh Main's riverside garden design (pages 152–5) are spot-on in this respect.

So (phew!), with a handle on the fundamentals — the jobs you want your plants to do and an appreciation of your climatic and soil factors — you can move forward.

While there are an infinite number of ways of combining plants for an equivalent number of reasons and purposes, there are some constants in planting design that remain, regardless of your climate type or location.

These essentially come down to the basics of all design: size, shape, form, colour, texture, balance, proportion, repetition, contrast and rhythm. Might sound like we're getting into complex territory, but a lot

Kangaroo paw (*Anigozanthos* sp.) (above) is useful in dry planting schemes. A garden designed by Hugh Main (right), uses a mix of drought-hardy exotic and native plants to great sculptural effect, proving that waterwise gardening can be dynamic and interesting. Jane Burke has used plants native to her local area in Victoria (far right), creating a garden that relates beautifully to where it is.

of these things are about intuition, and if you keep simplicity as your mantra things needn't get too overwhelming.

So it's back to that idea of being able to look at plants and recognize their inherent design qualities. Firstly, look at the overall size and shape of a plant, whether it be a groundcover, a shrub or a tree. It is tall or short? Exactly how high does it grow? Is it narrow or rounded? Though the labels on the plants in the nursery are an excellent start to get an idea of the mature size and shape of a plant, it can be difficult to fully appreciate what that means in reality when you're looking at a much younger potted version. Again, this is where your own diligence and research will pay off. If you can't find shots in books, try the Internet or ask your nurseryperson about any example they may know of in a nearby garden, house or park — botanical gardens can be a great resource for this.

Next, colour, and I consider this is a biggy. What is the colour of a plant's foliage? Yes it might be green, but what sort of green — grey-green, blue-green, lime-green or perhaps dark green? Beyond the greens, there's a host of reds, purples and silvers. Then there are flowers — the colour, shape and form available are virtually infinite.

Some plants will possess stronger characteristics than others. Some will be dominant in shape and form like succulents and so-called architectural plants: things with spiky or strappy leaves. Some will dazzle with the colour of their foliage and some will be impossible to miss because of the impressive size and shape of their leaves.

Texture too is an important classification — this can be appreciated either on an up-close, intimate scale, leaf by leaf, or by standing back

to get an overall impression. Things with small leaves will generally have a fine texture to them, while things with bigger leaves with have a rougher texture — this depends also on the stiffness, smoothness, softness and glossiness or mattness of the foliage.

Once you begin to see plants in this way you can assign them to their appropriate jobs in the garden and start thinking about making satisfying combinations and compositions. Creating a successful planting scheme is like creating a well-designed interior: elements complementing and blending with each other, with moments of drama and focus, to form a satisfying, stimulating composition.

So how do you determine whether plants will work with one another? There are any numbers of ways, but I find a good way is doing it via colour and texture. Grouping similarly coloured foliage (and flowers) together is relatively foolproof. Generally speaking, plants that have similar colour and texture (not flowers though) will work together because they've evolved in similar conditions and climates over many thousands of years. Silver-foliaged plants generally hail from dry climates, and glossy-green-foliaged plants mostly hail from tropical and subtropical — note that this is a massive generalization, but for the purpose of putting together a planting scheme a bit of like with like works wonders.

While it's easy to be seduced by the desire to fill up a planting scheme with flowers, don't do it at the expense of the body and structure of your planting scheme — flowers come and go (don't get the wrong idea, I'm a big flower fan), while a good planting scheme needs guts. Guts comes via a couple of things: those filler plants I was

talking about at the beginning of the chapter and the more structured plants strong in form and shape that aren't afraid to pull focus.

Whenever I've struggled trying to get a scheme to work, two single things have saved the day every time. First, pulling focus as I just mentioned, and second, employing the less is more philosophy — in fact, it should be more of less. Repeating the same plant en masse can be a very useful method of giving a scheme some consistency, strength and clarity. Overall leaf and plant shapes when repeated become blocks of colour and texture, creating greater impact and having a more profound presence within a garden. That is not to say that your entire garden should comprise just one type of plant, but this approach is good to apply to one area or a single planting bed.

The more of less method is enhanced greatly when you add a focus puller to really bring it all home. A boldly shaped succulent or even a pot containing something in dazzling flower will give a simple scheme much-needed focus, which will help to stitch it together visually.

The plant bit of your garden is the biggest variable, so don't be afraid of making mistakes, because you will make mistakes. Remember, this is another way of getting to know your garden — use the lessons from those mistakes to make it better.

Iresine herbstii (far left) produces a mass of intense, iridescent pink foliage that can be used to dramatic effect. The blue-green tones and sculptural form of a lone *Agave attenuata* (left) make a powerful focus adrift in a sea of the dark purple foliage of alternanthera. A mass of small grey-leafed *Cerastium tomentosum* (above) creates a finely textured groundcover.

HARD PALETTE

The colour and texture of the garden floor can have significant influence on the overall look and feel of a garden. When using something as highly patterned as stone flagging (far left), walls and other vertical elements should be plainer and smoother in appearance. Rust paint and rust-coloured natural reed cladding (left) make a contrasting textural but tonal combination.

GET CO-ORDINATED

You may have noticed that not once in this book have I used the word style. It's my little mission in garden life to dispense with preconceived, prepackaged notions of what gardens are meant to be. It's pretty hard not to talk in 'styles' — we're all conditioned to classify everything according to these — particularly in gardens. Tropical style, Balinese style, French style, the list goes on. When a style is transplanted holus bolus from somewhere else, beyond its native context, it can verge on the ridiculous. I'm in the business of encouraging the development of original, individual gardens that say more about the person that lives in them and where they are, than about what magazines the owner's been reading.

If elements particular to any of the 'style' families have some resonance and connection for you, by all means go for it. It's more a case of using these as sources of inspiration and lessons on design rather than as something to mimic.

But throw away all those easy-to-grasp style categories and what are we left with? It takes us back to the very essence of what makes gardens tick, the things that create the visual and sensual experiences that make gardens the spirited, inspiring places they can be. It's all about exploring colour and texture — the fundamental palette of garden making.

The way all colour and texture behaves via an infinite array of combinations and variations is at the root of how we experience anything — particularly in the garden. All sounds a bit intangible, but once you understand that you have the means to control, play with and guide these fundamental elements, then you begin to create some really exciting and sensually igniting garden spaces.

It's not too much of a stretch to appreciate that we can ultimately control an interior space to create precisely the mood we want. Paint, curtains, cushions, floor coverings, furniture can all be cobbled together with reasonable confidence. But step outside and that

confidence can quickly evaporate. I'm not talking about getting everything matching and things complementing each other so perfectly that you create the garden equivalent of a super-slick designer penthouse gracing the pages of a bi-monthly glossy. It's more about building towards an overall feeling of harmony, all your bits, plants and colours working with each other rather than against.

As far as colour in the garden is concerned, the immediate source to lock onto is flowers. Yes, but that is only one source. Every element of the garden can provide exciting colour opportunities. This is where it helps to consider the garden as a 'room' with walls, a floor, furniture and those extra things called plants. Beyond the flowers, a greater source of colour comes via foliage. For example, much of Australia's east coast is able to support a wide variety of colourful foliage plants ranging from the hot pinks of iresine to the subdued but moody black-purples of alocasia.

Remember that using colour doesn't just mean using lots of bright bold colours in the one space. Using colour effectively is more to do with controlling it and limiting it. A bold hot pink played out against a background of deep neutrals will have much greater impact than a collision of bright colours.

Colour can be introduced to (and controlled in) an outdoor space in a number of ways. Coloured walls (above) create a great foil for objects in front of them; foliage and flowers (right) are the most common way of using colour in the garden; screens and walls (top and bottom far right) made from unusual materials (here from Perspex and an old screen door) provide opportunities to add colour.

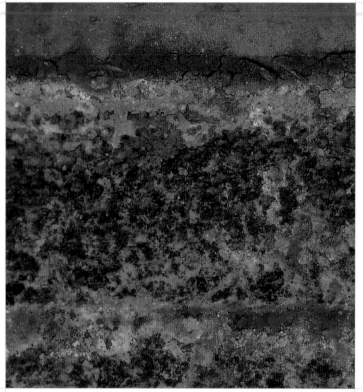

Playing with colour in the garden is probably a little easier to get your head around than texture. Everything has texture: rough or smooth, soft or hard. It's the thing that invites you to touch or warns you to keep clear. A texture will become most apparent when it's juxtaposed against its opposite: a rough texture will stand out much more effectively next to a serenely smooth one. Getting control of texture is usually about paring back and simplifying. Too many textures in the one space can be overwhelming.

Plants aside, the base texture in the garden comes via the hard elements: the walls, fences and floors, and even mulches.

The simplest way to get an idea of whether your proposed combination of materials is going to work or clash is to place samples together — your pebbles, timber samples, paint colours and so on — creating a palette board. Interior designers do this, and it works just as well for the garden. It will help you avoid the common mistake of using too many textures next to one another. It's more about the contrasts between a handful of well-chosen materials than using all of your favourites in the one garden.

Certain materials have the power to take your garden in different directions both mood- and feel-wise. Timber and stone, for example,

Materials with unique texture and colour: (clockwise from above) the rich earthy patina of rust; the horizontal lines of timber cladding in deep dirty purple; the gold and cream tones of sandstone; the earthy softness of decomposed granite against the soft neutral tones of exposed-aggregate concrete; the silver of weathered hardwood; and the rich browns of stacked stone.

will generally 'warm up' a space because of their earthy organic origins — Carol White's garden 'Lavandula' (pages 138–41) is a classic example of the power of timber and stone combined. Add highlights of stainless steel or aluminium as in the pergola structures in the suburban gardens of both Scott and Renae (pages 96–107) and Jeff and Michele (pages 126–37) and the palette of materials is given a modern edge.

The garden floor is as important as any component, and just like the floors inside your home, can be make or break. For me, the material chosen for the ground plane is one of the most powerful in dictating the feel of the garden. The best way to grasp this idea is to look at all the gardens in this book and try the following exercise: where there is decomposed granite (for example, Geoff and Lindy's beachside garden, pages 142–51) — imagine it replaced with brick paving. Where there is gravel (Jeff and Michele's reinvented suburban garden, pages 126–37), try and imagine it turfed. In all instances the garden would be radically altered.

STYLING

When it comes to styling — less is best. Woven-cane drum chairs (far left) and large aubergine floor cushions are all that are needed to create a chilled comfortable atmosphere on a weatherproof verandah. Retro wire furniture (left) can work well in a variety of garden types.

THE ESSENTIAL FLOURISH

Styling is big business these days. Stylists bring to the aesthetically challenged garden or interior what the spin-doctors bring to the politician's re-election campaign: a lot of smoke and mirrors with a dash of truth for good measure.

It's the layer on top, the icing on the cake, the fun bit. Pay close attention to all those mouth-watering images from the glossy lifestyle magazines and you'll notice that the things that really set those gardens on fire are the cushions, the furniture and the odd well-chosen pot or piece of sculpture.

With so many boutique garden centres and the big mega 'everything you'll ever need under one roof' lifestyle stores proliferating these days, the choice of garden accessories you can add to your space is mind boggling. The range is so vast that while they make terrific final flourishes to a spunky garden, they can also resurrect the most average of back yards.

The thing to bear in mind as with all aspects of design is to err on the side of simplicity. It doesn't take much for a space to feel overdone or overstyled. 'Less is more' should guide you all the way here. While adding the final touches is definitely a fun aspect of garden making, the bits and pieces that you use will also often be character-defining — particularly in the case of sculpture.

Outdoor furniture is probably one of the biggest wants in this department and it's also one of the things that will either take a space to the next level or just kill it. Sure, it's got to be comfortable and durable, but a lot of the furniture that's working overtime to satisfy these factors can be pretty average in the aesthetics department. In my book, it's critical for furniture to be in scale with the space it's in, and made of a material that works with the garden as much as any other element. The smaller the space, the finer the furniture should be. Wire or cane furniture works well in smaller spaces, while big bulky teak furniture is most at home in substantially proportioned gardens.

My personal obsession in furniture is the older, retro 1950s and 60s wire pieces that take well to a wide variety of spaces, combined with old, rundown timber tables and chairs — a look that I never tire of.

More and more, however, there are some amazing pieces of outdoor furniture coming onto the market — stunning contemporary examples made from plastic, metal and timber and other positively space age materials. Many of them are jaw-droppingly bold or sublimely beautiful sculptural pieces in their own right — and most come with a jaw-dropping price tag to match. If you can afford it, go crazy, and take comfort in the knowledge that most of these are designer pieces that are investments for life.

Pots are the next essential styling item that every garden tends to benefit from. I never fail to be amazed how a garden I've worked on just catapults to another level when well-chosen pots and accompanying plants are placed around it. They help to bring dead corners to life, define entrances and passageways and create dynamic still lifes in their own right, pulling focus and stealing the show every single time.

In choosing and arranging pots there are a few little rules to live by. Firstly go for a few bigger pots rather than a plethora of small ones. It gives you fewer things to keep alive and creates greater impact. Keep the majority of your pots simple in shape and low on sheen and decoration. Ornate, decoratively shaped and glazed pots should be used sparingly, as these have a habit of stealing focus — essentially it should be the plants that are being featured as opposed to the pots.

I myself have a penchant for metal and concrete pots, both contemporary pieces and those hailing from the 1950s and 60s — can't get enough of them!

One of the real joys of pots is that they can be like the furniture in the lounge room that you move around every few months on a rainy Sunday afternoon. Though you're better off shifting pots when the weather's a little less inclement, you can experiment with all manner of compositions. Useful pots for such tableaux are tall skinny pots and low-slung bowls. The tall ones add much-needed height and are best kept to the rear. The low-slung bowls help to anchor and ground the taller and medium height containers and add a sense of foreground to your compositions.

Cushions and candles are the things you can throw around to your heart's content. If you develop a taste for the built-in seat or daybed, investing in a pile of cushions is an absolute necessity. The placing of the cushions at my share place is something of a summer ritual now. A custom-made cushion from an upholsterer for the daybed-come-sandpit in my garden (pages 64–75) piled high with cushions makes for the most prized spot in the house or garden for a good four to five months of the year.

Top of the range — sleek contemporary designer furniture (far left) makes a sublime statement. Pieces like this are lifetime investments. Concrete pots made during the 1950s and 60s (left and above) come in great shapes with funky graphic patterning; they make excellent partners for succulents and cacti.

The garden ceiling is something to exploit (also as per my own back yard) and something that is often overlooked. Cables or chains strung up from tree to house, or tree to tree, can be hung with lights, ranging in style from Chinese paper lanterns through to elaborate candelabras. These lend a great festive mood to the garden. Adding a 'ceiling' to your space takes the outdoor room concept to another level altogether.

Sculpture is a highly personal element in the garden — or at least it should be. Sculpture is your chance to add something to the garden that says something about you, something about where you are and maybe something about where you've been. I myself am a fan of sculpture that doesn't scream 'I'm a piece of garden sculpture!' Sculpture specifically made for the garden, like the ubiquitous water feature, has captured the imagination of many an industrious artist and these days there are a huge range of pieces available, some of them great, some not so. But sculpture, of all the elements of the garden, is enormously subjective and what is one person's 'David' is another person's pile of rubbish. From my experience, however, the best sculpture is stuff that gets people talking — either heatedly or else in rapturous tones.

The craypots (above) in Jane Burke's Victorian garden were found washed up on nearby beaches. Their bulbous form mimics the tufts of native grasses among which they hide. These steel reinforcement rod and timber sculptures (right) echo the trunks of the surrounding eucalypt forest. The wire balls (far right) form a delicate, unimposing sculpture.

After choice of sculpture comes placement. This depends largely on the sculpture itself and the impact you want to make. Jane Burke's restored bushland garden (pages 184–7) is a case study in subtlety — the craypots echo the form of the grasses they're tucked under, and the collections of flotsam and jetsam washed up onto the nearby coast are casually, but artistically, strewn so you discover them only when you take the time to explore the garden.

The wire balls in Lou and Anthony's mountain garden (pages 172–83) are a bolder more apparent placement, but because they have a transparency to them they gently animate the garden rather than dominate it.

One measure of success for any styling item is that if you were to remove it from the space, it would feel like something was missing from the garden, which would look a little barer. If the garden looks better for its removal, then it may have been one extra too many in the first place!

PART 2 MOAR GARDENS AND
INSPIRATION

A GARDEN FOR THE MOST GROWN-UP OF SHARE HOUSES, A SPACE THAT'S INTIMATE AND WARM, CONDUCIVE TO GOOD TIMES AND LONG HOURS OF CONVERSATION, A MOOD ENHANCED BY RICH COLOUR AND EARTHY MATERIALS

MOAR GARDEN 1

(CO)OPERATION GARDEN

Speaking as a young (ish) person, buying a house these days sucks. The prices aren't just expensive — they're obscene. To avoid a lifetime of crippling debt you either make do with a depressing little shoebox or else move a long, long, long way from the middle of anywhere. Would you like a garden with that? Now you're just being silly!

For those of us who really value some type of garden space, it's a frustrating dilemma. Faced with this dilemma, three close friends and I thought that rather than give up and live in a gloomy bed-sit in some far-flung destination it made sense for us to band together, join financial forces and take control. We wanted to live in a certain area, with a back yard, and the only way we could do it was together.

Discussing this whole concept with friends, family and acquaintances we got all sorts of responses. From You're mad, right through to It makes perfect sense! Well it made perfect sense to us. We'd lived together in various share houses for the last ten years, been through all sorts of ups and downs, and made it through unscathed.

Once we made the decision to do it, it became an adventure, an exciting new life chapter for us all, and after renting and living in share houses for so long the whole idea of buying a house felt very grown up.

Following some very official meetings we set ourselves on a course of action. Luckily, after a relatively short, pain-free search we found the house in just the right spot with almost the right number of bedrooms and the all-important back yard. But not a back yard of the proportions and type — lots of grass surrounded by a paling fence — that we normally think of as a back yard in Australia. It was more of a courtyard — a space around 7 x 12 metres (23 x 40 feet) with a garage taking up a quarter of it.

Beyond actually having some sort of outdoor space, the biggest plus that the place had going for it was the already established connection between inside and out. Floor to ceiling french doors that spanned the width of the building set up that all important indoor/outdoor flow — the sort of flow that sets the real estate copywriter's heart aflutter.

With the exception of a couple of so-so trees — a fiddlewood (*Citharexylum spinosum*) that dropped half a metre (a foot's worth) of leaves every day (or so it seemed) — and wall-to-wall coloured concrete paving that we weren't crazy about, the space had great bones.

COLOUR

Although the overall effect is an abundance of colour, bright hot colours (in large expanses) have been avoided. The main expanses of colour — the purple painted building, the blue-green of the lavender and the pale ochre tones of the garden floor — are in muted shades. The combination of these colours creates a 'base' for small contrasting highlights of hot pink (the edge of the circular window and the *Iresine herbstii* planted at the base of the wall) and white (the candles) to bring the colour scheme to life. Before committing to large areas of painted colour always experiment with small tester pots: it will save time, money and your relationship with fellow householders!

CUES, CLUES, IDEAS, ELEMENTS, INSPIRATION
DEEP SATURATED COLOUR INTIMACY BLUISH-GREEN DIRTY PURPLE
WEATHERED TIMBER LET THE CONVERSATION FLOW
ESCAPE CELEBRATE CONGREGATE

It's a bit of a cliché that you should live in a place for at least twelve months before doing anything to the garden. I was finding this little rule pretty hard to adhere to but due to circumstances beyond my control I had to hold my horses.

This, as it turned out, was a blessing in disguise. Biding your time allows you to just live in a place and get used to its rhythms and all the factors that influence it. A lot of things can only float to the surface over time — over months — and if you dive in head first you can find yourself doing things that you might regret later on. Perhaps the most valuable thing to get a handle on is precisely how the sun and shade shift and change over the full range of seasons.

The circumstances beyond my control basically boiled down to the fact that when you have four decision-making adults (as opposed to two) things tend to move a little slower. Even though I tend to muscle forward when it comes to the garden department, everyone still puts in their two cents worth. Sounds like it could be a nightmare but we, as a bunch, are pretty good at getting through the awkward moments and, without fail, manage to turn it into joke fodder.

Naturally I had some pretty strong ideas on where we should head. The thing that binds us as a group is that we all like our living spaces to be warm and intimate. Cups of tea and well-made coffee flow constantly from our kitchen, so the main thing the garden needed to be was a place where we could absorb all this caffeine into our bloodstream as comfortably as possible.

Working in the world of gardens, I see a lot of different garden spaces — big, small, fat and thin. Without fail the ones that I always go gaga over are the ones with that elusive soul factor — the ones that look like they hold stories and dear memories for all those who've been a part of them. A garden with a rickety old table shaded by a one hundred year old grape vine, surrounded by stone paving and an assortment of rusty decaying treasures is my idea of heaven. That fantasy firmly in mind, we had quite a challenge in front of us.

The problem in creating your own garden when you're an obsessive garden freak like me is that you almost go mad as you come up with the fifty-seventh concept review of the back yard. I kept this overload of ideas to myself, as disclosing them to the rest of the house would have sent our design panel approval process into meltdown. A better approach was to reveal it in bite-sized pieces.

First bite-sized piece was the deck, which developed from the need to incorporate the garage in the design. One of the best features of the space, something that gave the back yard its good bones, was the garage. It created a great potential backdrop to the whole garden. As it stood, however, it seemed ungrounded as it loomed over the courtyard. The 'leftover' space that ran down its length created a long narrow area that would never be used. The solution was to put in a deck that matched the floor level of the garage, effectively grounding the structure. The addition of the deck had an unexpected benefit, turning the main body of the courtyard into a 'central' space which really felt like it was on the way to becoming the heart of the house as opposed to just the space out the back.

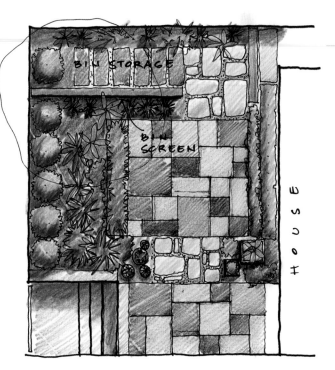

FRONT GARDEN

The overall concept was to create a range of ways of spending time in the garden and a sense of being engulfed by foliage.

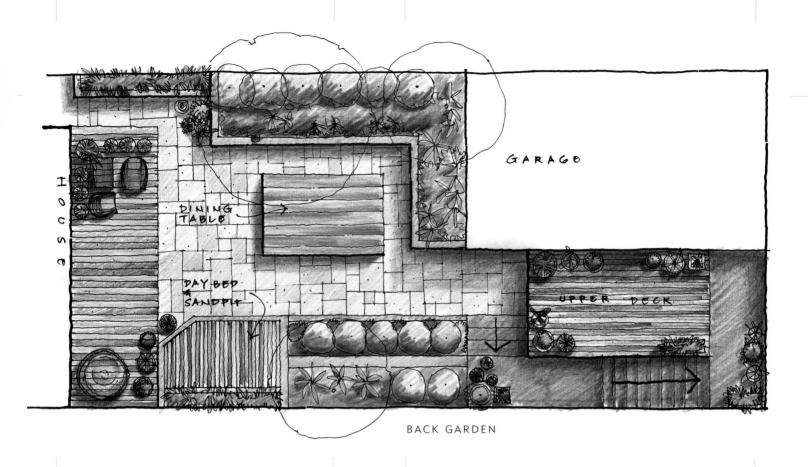

BACK GARDEN

KEY PLANTS

TREES
Lagerstroemia indica
    (Crepe myrtle)
Plumeria lutea
    (Yellow frangipani)

BLUE-GREEN/GREY-GREEN FOLIAGE
Euphorbia wulfenii subsp.
    characias (Spurge)
Festuca glauca
    (Blue fescue)
Lavandula x *allardii*
    (Allard's French lavender)
Metrosideros thomasii
    (NZ Christmas bush)
Pittosporum tenuifolium
    'Silver Sheen'

PURPLE-PINK FOLIAGE
Canna 'Tropicana'
Iresine herbstii
Tradescantia pallida

FOCAL POINT
Agave attenuata
    (Century plant)

PRIVACY SCREENER
Bambusa oldhamii

FEATURE PLANTS
Anigozanthos 'Bushranger'
    (Kangaroo paw)
Drepanostachyum falcatum
    (Himalayan weeping
    bamboo)

PLANTS USED IN POTS
Buxus microphylla
    (Japanese box)
Dracaena tricolor
Liriope muscari 'Evergreen
    Giant'

The material we used for the deck was all reused timber. Huge sections of hardwood became the posts. It was a good lesson for me to go to the extra effort of sourcing interesting timber. Had we just used regular treated pine posts the effect and feel would have been totally different. The timber certainly set the garden on the path of securing that soul factor I was so determined to capture.

The next step was a combination of spontaneous ideas/solutions and lengthy contemplation regarding the space located at the back doors. Sheltered by the first floor balcony, this space looked like a verandah but for some reason didn't feel like one, and for the life of me I couldn't figure out why it wasn't working.

As soon as we moved in we set up a couple of chairs and a table in anticipation of it being a great tea and chat spot. At our previous house we had a similar set-up in what seemed a similar location and so were keen to replicate it. Eventually I worked out it was a matter of scale and proportion. The success of the tea and chat spot at our previous house was due to the verandah roof being fairly low, keeping the scale intimate. But the first floor deck that created the ceiling to our new spot was almost twice the height of our old verandah. I found two ways to help rectify this. Firstly, I had to bring down the height of the 'ceiling', so I suspended some cheap bamboo blinds from the beam that supported the first floor balcony. Secondly, I needed to create a sense of a verandah-like space by making some delineation at ground level. As it stood, the coloured concrete paving ran all the way up to the back door. Driving past a nearby building site I saw a skip full of discarded paling fence panels. I had a blinding flash and realized that they would be the perfect thing to simply lay on the concrete at the back door to create a 'floor' for the verandah. As soon as they were laid in place there was a dramatic change. The floor created a special space and gave the real feeling of a verandah at the back door: that great intermediate space between out and in where you feel safe and secure, where you can watch the world go by — or in our case, watch a garden come together.

With these key spatial issues pretty much resolved it was on to the fun stuff — turning this space into a haven. The focus now was on creating places to sit and relax while being engulfed by greenery, colour and texture. In a garden this size it's important to strike the right balance between people and plants. It's one thing to have a garden full of prized bromeliads, but if you can't loll around them, up close and personal, you're missing out on the best sorts of interaction that garden spaces can offer — not forgetting of course the interactions between people in gardens.

It meant trying to create a range of ways of spending time in the garden — and this simply comes down to ways of sitting or lying in the space. It was clear from the moment we moved into this place that the focus of the garden was going to be the lovely old table that was a roadside find years before. A dining table surrounded by chairs, then, was one reason for being in the garden. The second was the now improved and operational tea and chat spot at the back door. It was time to create the third and contrasting way of being in the garden. The answer? A daybed of course! They're a bit of a 'now' inclusion in the garden but when done well (in terms of position, orientation and size) they're fantastic.

This daybed was to be built-in, so it was important to get it right. In combination with the construction of the daybed, new raised planting beds were built around the perimeter of the garden to provide somewhere to create the plant engulfment the space was begging for. Before building the planting beds, it hadn't been far off wall-to-wall concrete.

One other issue to address was the access door to the large storage room that occupied the ground level portion of the garage. It opened directly into the middle of the space and meant that it was all about the door into the storage room. The locations of these sorts of access points or thoroughfares need to be well thought-out as they can seriously compromise a space. Shifting the door around to the side of the building, underneath the deck, meant a planting bed could now be created in front of the garage wall. This wall could become a real backdrop to the whole space and in particular to the planting directly in front of it.

So with the brick planters and daybed in position the structure of the garden was in place. The daybed also happens to double as a sandpit. The timber deck top comes off, albeit with the brute strength of two men. Note to self, make that lighter next time. It is easy to incorporate sandpits in small spaces, where they can be disguised as something else all together. The key is making access to them easy and manageable by one person — particularly a mum.

The position of a built-in seat has to be given careful consideration. They should have a subtlety about them and work with the other built elements in the garden like the house, walls and planter beds. There needs to be a design logic. Daybeds in particular need to be surrounded by other seating, preferably unfixed so that it feels like you have some flexibility. If it's all working properly, your built-in seating should be the thing that everyone dives for — pole position! Ours is close to the back door, hard up against the verandah, the spot where people naturally gravitate. If it were at the back corner I don't think it would be as successful.

The other killer factor making it the most prized spot in the garden is the option for it to be shaded. While it's great to have a daybed in a spot that gets winter sun, let's face it, you'll spend most time on it during summer — and there is nothing worse than having no shade over summer. A simple timber canopy 'floats' over the daybed, with another inexpensive bamboo blind attached to dowel and strung along stainless steel cables. This was actually hastily thrown together in a few hours one Christmas eve in readiness for Christmas lunch. One of these days I plan to get it re-made out of aluminium as it's lightweight but stronger and better able to cope with the high tension cables, which will not pull it out of shape.

So enough of the building blocks, what of the colour and movement? This garden to me is a great example of the power of colour and in particular the power of paint.

When we moved in, this place was painted head to toe in cream and heritage green. A popular colour combination, but it's a little dated and quite frankly I don't think it does you a lot of favours. I'm still to be convinced that pale colours and white are truly useful in the garden. They're glarey and washed out, and the common claim that they make space look bigger outdoors is in my outspoken opinion . . . dubious.

There is a colour I have fallen in love with over the last few years as well as a type of paint. A finely textured variety, beautiful stuff, which works so well because of its super flat quality. It reflects no light whatsoever, meaning it completely absorbs light, giving the colour a beautiful, soft, saturated quality. It settles and grounds the objects and surfaces it's painted on, which makes it a perfect foil for foliage as there is no competition between the painted surface and the plants — with perfectly matt paint, it becomes all about the plant.

The colour in question is pumpernickel. It's a beautiful, deep, dirty purple. This colour almost operates as a neutral, working with a wide range of colours: blues, greens, greys and browns, through to reds and pinks. Painting the garage and other walls in pumpernickel had a dramatic impact on the space. Suddenly the things that were important were the things in front of the colour — the plants, the timbers, the ornaments and even the people! The shape and form of everything comes to the fore in front of a deep colour.

Planting out this garden has been an ongoing process. Again I find it difficult to live by the advice I so easily foist upon others. The basic idea was to plant the sides of the space with something simple

PRIVACY ISSUES

Lack of privacy can often be one of the main reasons an outdoor space is not used to its full potential. There are two ways to deal with it. First, you can extend the vertical height of your fences with some type of planting or screen, as per the bamboo behind the daybed (shown opposite). Alternatively — and this is the more unusual method — you can block the view into your space with a horizontal canopy, like the overhead bamboo blind above the daybed. A retractable canopy like this means that even if you are next to a tall block of flats you can easily maintain your privacy without having to build or grow outrageously high vertical screens.

The daybed (left) is shaded by both the retractable bamboo blind awning and the overhanging branches of a young crepe myrtle (out of shot left). The bamboo (*Bambusa oldhamii*) is echoed by a chalk drawing on the purple wall by artist Adam Jones, while the timber lid of the daybed conceals a sandpit. *Agave attenuata* (above) draw focus among the hot pinks of *Iresine herbstii*.

and neutral — *Pittosporum tenuifolium* 'Silver Sheen' along the fences, with Allard's French lavender sitting in front. These built up a base palette of blue-green foliage that worked as a beautiful soft contrast to the purple walls, and acted as a foil for the riot of hot pinks and reds that were to sit in the bed in front of the purple garage backdrop. The pinks and reds came via iresine and canna lilies plus the odd surviving kangaroo paw (*Anigozanthos* species). The kangaroo paws are a good example of my irresponsible horticultural behaviour — committing them to certain death as I plant them against a south-facing wall that receives little if any sun whatsoever. I know it's terrible but I can't help it, I just find them irresistible. To allay my guilt I try to think of them more as potted colour.

The evolution part of the planting scheme has come about through more death. Namely the lavender — it did well for a couple of seasons, but then decided that things were starting to get a bit too shady. Eventually it had to come out. In its place I'm trying *Euphorbia characias* subsp. *wulfenii* (spurge). Doesn't give me quite as lovely a dense mass of blue-grey as the lavender did, but it's not too far off. Their lime-green flowerheads during spring are luminescent against the dirty purple and blues in the garden. The tradescantia and lime green sedum at the base of the euphorbia create a great tumble of colour that doesn't compete with the concentration of hot pinks and reds in the bed against the purple garage wall.

Good old agaves, those slightly passé succulents, do a great job in small spaces of creating focus in a planting scheme and bringing a sense of strength that grounds the scheme without letting it to get too fluffy. Take care when placing agaves. Because they are so strong in form and shape, they can be the difference between a well-balanced composition or one that feels like it's lost its way. Agaves and similarly tufted or ball-like forms, including grasses, work well when placed at the base of trees or at the corners of buildings or planting beds.

Small spaces owe much to the finishing touches, and that generally means pots. It never ceases to amaze me that while you can go to great lengths, effort and expense to create or rework a garden in terms of the overall layout and configuration, in the end the things that really make it and steal the show are the pots. They bring dead corners to life, create focal points and allow the garden to take on infinite variations to its look depending on the type of pots, what's growing in them and where they are positioned.

I've been building up my own collection of pots over the years, and I've been through a few phases. I've got plenty of the regular terracotta variety, a few roadside finds, a range of metal bits and pieces and of late, retro concrete. However, a variety I've always steered away from are glazed pots. Glossy objects, like glossy painted surfaces, are the first things to attract the eye, so I'm a big believer in using glazed pots sparingly. They behave like a feature plant or object, and work to great effect in shady corners if you're trying to inject a bit of life into them.

The finishing touch that really took this space to another level was the chandelier. The sense of a ceiling in an outdoor space is a simple

BLUE AND PURPLE FOLIAGE

There are innumerable ways of creating a planting scheme, but one favourite method of mine is to build up a base of plants with blue-green and grey-green foliage and then add purple-foliaged plants as a contrast. Succulents and lavender are great for blue-green and grey-green effects, as are many grasses such as *Festuca glauca*. Favourite purples are *Tradescantia pallida* and *Alternanthera ficoidea*. Then there are the plants that combine both blue and purple in the one leaf — blue-green on the top with a purple underside like *Rhoeo spathacea* and *Ctenanthe setosa*.

A collection of succulents including echeveria (top far left) have permanent residency on the timber table. The garden owes much to streetside finds including the old timber ladder and pot hanger — (centre far left). *Agave attenuata* and *Tradescantia pallida* (bottom far left) create a great blue-green and purple combination. The coloured foliage of the red-and-black-striped New Zealand flax (left, seen at left of shot) and *Dracaena tricolor* contrast against the blue of *Festuca glauca* and the lime green foliage of black bamboo.

enough thing to achieve, but it's something people often neglect exploiting. Stringing a chain from house to deck creates a support for anything from Chinese paper lanterns to sheets of muslin for impromptu shade. Hanging the chandelier from the chain takes the outdoor room concept almost as far it can go. The chandelier and table together make a very complete and satisfying picture — so much so that if one or both are now removed for some reason, the garden looks like something is definitely missing and it's not quite feeling itself.

Our little front garden is the most recent addition to our house. It was previously a great burglar deterrent with its termite-ridden heritage green paling fence. As well as being an embarrassment, the fence was becoming a public nuisance as passers-by dodged falling palings that crumbled away on a daily basis.

Front yards have a tough time. They are the neglected sibling in the garden's family of spaces. The back yard gets all the attention and is where all the action happens. But just like the cover of this book, the front yard is what your home may very well be judged by.

We returned our front yard to a clean slate by removing a large melaleuca planted right over the water mains and a couple of metrosideroses in poor condition. The key things were to continue the feel achieved via the palette of colour and texture in the back yard, and to find a way of dealing with those necessary uglies known as rubbish and compost bins.

A new fence made from simple rectangular treated pine palings running vertically was a nice clean option, while exactly the same palings running horizontally extended the height of the neighbouring fence. The other elements that would give this small front space a little extra zing came from a secondhand building centre. Two old flyscreen doors, featuring metal scrolls and curls — the type of door that made that familiar creaky 'thwack' in your grandparents' falling-down beach shack — begged to be taken home and were clearly destined for greater things. Removing the tatty fly gauze and associated staples, handles and hinges left two lovely screens with all sorts of possibilities. Sanding back the timber frames, painting them the familiar dirty purple and coating the metal scrolls with copper-look paint transformed the screens. One was destined for the front gate, the other to be part of a solid screen to hide the bins.

Continuing the dirty purple onto the front of the house was a logical decision and meant the same palette of plants could be used. Playing with the purple and blue foliage established in the back garden, a mix of purple-leafed heuchera, purple tradescantia and the handy blue grass *Festuca glauca* make up a complementary carpet of colour and texture. Again, agaves give structure and focus to the whole scheme, with the addition this time of a cycad. A hedge of buxus along the front verandah wall also adds some welcome structure. It's important to balance the loose and unstructured plants with strong uncomplicated forms. A lot more sun in the front yard meant silver- and blue-foliaged plants could be used with more confidence, namely a shrub version of the New Zealand Christmas bush, *Metrosideros* species. This has beautiful silver new foliage and is

RETRO CONCRETE POTS

During the 1950s and 60s pots were commonly made from concrete. Lighter weight terracotta eventually took over as the favoured material for containers, and pots are now made from a wide range of materials including plastic and metal, in all shapes and sizes. Today concrete pots are regaining favour for their unusual shapes and patterns. Original concrete pots from the 1950s and 60s are quickly becoming collector's items, and while some of them are incredibly ugly, others come in great shapes and incorporate some very funky patterns and textures. For some reason succulents seem to make great plant partners for concrete pots. Scour secondhand shops, auction houses and the Internet for some great finds.

quite a sight when covered in its pom-pom like bright red flowers. Out here my otherwise poorly treated beauties, kangaroo paws, could actually live more than six weeks, and dare I say it, flourish.

An old landscape architect boss of mine once told me how his old architect boss told him the secret of making an entry memorable and creating an impression on the visitor. The secret, he said, was to put all your energy into the door handle. This is the one thing the visitor is compelled to interact with, and if it's whiz-bang, they won't forget it. While the door handle on our front door is pretty straight up and down, I figured the next best thing was to paint it in an unforgettable colour — the hot pink door in high gloss now makes a thumping contrast against the dirty purple. Front doors are a great case for glossy paint finishes. They're the most durable of finishes and when contrasted against super flat paints the effect is dazzling.

The paving is a great example of making sense of a whole lot of leftover bits and pieces. I had a few concrete pavers and a whole bunch of sandstone offcuts left over from other jobs and was determined to put them to use in the front and make it look as if the result was intentional rather than accidental and ad hoc. The way to do it, I discovered, was to put like with like. Square or rectangular pads of sandstone alternating with similar pads of concrete pavers, build up a pretty sophisticated-looking patchwork of paving.

With the front yard complete, it is a matter of waiting for the planting to grow and develop to catch up with the sanctuary-like feel of the back yard. Both front and back spaces are now richly coloured and textured places that say welcome, make yourself at home.

Welcome to Jack's house! The hot pink door creates a memorable entrance (far left). The colour scheme and planting in the front garden (top left) continue the approach adopted in the back garden. The metal scroll screen (above left), an old screen door built into a low dividing wall, was incorporated to provide somewhere to hide the rubbish bins. Retro pots (top right) are used throughout the garden.

A MOSAIC GARDEN

CREATIVE SPIRIT

DESIGNED BY MARGOT KNOX

FROM A GARDEN THAT HAS EVOLVED THROUGH THE SPIRIT OF CO-OPERATION AND SHARING, TO A GARDEN THAT EXPRESSES PURE CREATIVE SPIRIT AND SHARES IT WITH ALL WHO ENTER

The garden is crammed full of hidden details such as the ceramic rose (below left). Margot used a combination of blue and white tiles at the base of the walls to 'ground' the design. As she progressed up the wall she was free to become more adventurous with her colour combinations. It's hard to compete with the mosaic for attention and it seems the only plants that can hold their own are succulents, plants with strong sculptural forms such as the *Agave attenuata* (right) and *Aeonium arboreum* 'Zwartkop' (centre far right).

Margot Knox's mosaic garden is quite simply my favourite garden in the whole wide world. The first moment I entered it, it literally took my breath away. I've been back on a number of occasions now, and I'm still left short of breath every time.

Everything in this magical garden is covered in mosaic — and I mean everything. If it doesn't have blood or chlorophyll coursing through its veins, it's covered in mosaic.

While you might be familiar with the imagery of this much photographed and published garden, it still doesn't prepare you for the sensation when you physically set foot inside its walls. This place exudes a spirit unlike any garden, home or interior I've ever had the pleasure of visiting. When every square inch of a place has been pored over with such love, care and creativity, it's only natural that it is imbued with the energy of that process.

Margot, who passed away in 2002, was a little doer. Trained as a sculptor and painter, she was born with the building bug, as was her late husband, renowned architect Alistair Knox. Margot and Alistair were part of a movement of like-minded folk, including Gordon Ford (father of the Australian bush school of gardening), who sought to establish an alternative community in Eltham on Melbourne's fringe. There, during the 1950s, they designed and built their own (beautiful) mud brick and stone homes.

Working as the offsider of Ellis Stone (a renowned landscape designer famous for his stonework) to earn extra money while still a student, Margot became proficient in the art of laying stone floors and paving. The patience and diligence this sort of work demands clearly stood her in good stead for the creation of her mosaic garden.

It was 1985 when Alistair and Margot moved to East Hawthorn and took ownership of an old church hall, which was tired and in need of love, reeling from its 1960s overhaul, complete with glossy red air-conditioning ducting and acid green shag pile carpet.

Margot began work on the mosaic garden following Alistair's death in 1986. Up until that point, the upper courtyard — which is now the mosaic garden — hadn't received any real attention. Suddenly, however, following the installation of a secondhand bay window in the new guest room, there was a view into what was at the time a pretty drab old space. Margot subsequently set about rectifying this; and, always practical, concluded that if ever someone were to use the small courtyard they'd need somewhere to sit. So Margot and son Alistair fashioned a settee out of chicken wire and concrete — her favourite building materials. In finishing it off Margot decided that tiles would be as good a surface as any. And with that Margot was hooked.

Over the next few years, Margot — with the aid of her four sons and her daughter — applied mosaic to every surface in the garden. Low retaining walls were built, plus paths, steps and some creature-like pots mimicking the form of the succulents they were about to accommodate. There is even a tablecloth that has had the mosaic treatment.

Margot developed a few techniques and theories as she gradually became expert in this intricate art. Blue and white created 'a certain energy' and seemed to work well as a base on the walls. As Margot moved up the wall she realized she was free to go in any direction with colour and pattern — always, though, working to a loose design in her head. In order to give the whole design a sense of cohesion Margot would often 'embroider' ceramic flowers over the top, knitting the whole scheme together and giving it some consistency of pattern.

Any plants in this garden need to be wild and rambunctious if they are to steal attention away from the mosaic. There are big, bold, leafy things like banana palms with their lairy lime-green trunks, agaves with numerous whorled heads of fleshy foliage thrashing and whirling around each other, strelitzias that let loose a flurry of orange and purple when they decide to flower, and a plentiful supply of weird and gangly succulents. Luckily, none of these plants look like they're ready to be tamed.

Sitting in this garden, mesmerized by the flicker and shimmer of pattern and colour, you fall under its spell, dreaming what it must have been like to build it, to imagine it, to live in it. This is a garden that has a thousand stories to tell, and thousands more as you reflect on the past lives of every piece of tile that line these walls — and if you listen hard enough, Margot might just tell you some of them.

The installation of the aquamarine bay window (left) in the rear guest room was the catalyst for the creation of the mosaic garden. Everything is covered in mosaic including the tablecloth (top right). Margot used chicken wire and cement to create many of the elements in the garden, including the planters that mimic the form of the flamboyantly shaped plants they contain (centre right). A path leads to a unique garden shed (bottom right).

The southern garden is an enclosed space, surrounded by eighty-year-old windbreaks and trees. It owes its influence to the romanticized English garden ideal, full of perennials

A LARGE COUNTRY GARDEN EVER-CONSCIOUS OF ITS CONNECTION TO THE OUTER LANDSCAPE, A PLACE WITH TRADITIONAL BEGINNINGS AND CONTEMPORARY CONCLUSIONS, BLENDING FLORAL PROFUSION WITH A MORE RESTRAINED MODERN PALETTE, INFORMED BY ITS RURAL SURROUNDS

GARDEN IN A LANDSCAPE

Something I always ask other garden designers is how they got hooked on this whole garden thing. Invariably it happened somewhere below age twelve, in the veggie patch with a grandparent. Even though both my grandfathers were legendary veggie gardeners, I'm pretty certain my addiction didn't begin there.

No, I'm certain, my interest in gardens developed by default. Solely thanks to my finely honed skills of task avoidance. While studying for my final school exams (somewhere back in the mid 1980s), to get my brain into gear I'd have to watch a good three to four hours of daytime TV. Once the final strains of the 'Days of Our Lives' theme kicked in, I needed to balance my study preparation with some exterior activities — rummaging through the garden seemed as good a task as any. This, I'm sure, is where it all started.

Though photography captivated me for my first couple of years beyond school, I eventually came back to the garden thing when I began my degree in Landscape Architecture at the University of New South Wales in Sydney.

At the same time, mum and dad moved to 'Tamarang', a property located out of Armidale, New South Wales, and built a new house in the middle of 100 acres (about 40 hectares) perched atop a bald windy hill. It was the blankest of canvases and in my holidays from university we set about creating a garden. This was a huge learning curve for all of us: the biggest bit was establishing trust between me and mum and dad.

The exciting thing about building new gardens is how quickly you get results. Piles of dirt and rubbish, after much backbreaking work, transmogrify into planting beds that to the creators seem like works of art. Then when things are planted and actually begin growing, the satisfaction (particularly when it's your first time!) is really a most unexpected sensation.

In five years we managed to transform a completely bald hill into a garden. Though young, it was a garden definitely on its way to developing into a beautiful series of leafy spaces.

In 1993 I surprised myself by not being surprised at all by a phone call from dad to see how I'd feel if they were to move on from 'Tamarang'. 'Que sera sera' was my reply, if I remember correctly.

CUES, CLUES, IDEAS, ELEMENTS, INSPIRATION
UNDULATING LANDFORMS ROMANCE FLORAL DELIGHT
CONTRASTING SPACES BEYOND THE FENCELINE DISTANT HORIZONS
SILVERS AND GREYS OCHRES AND REDS

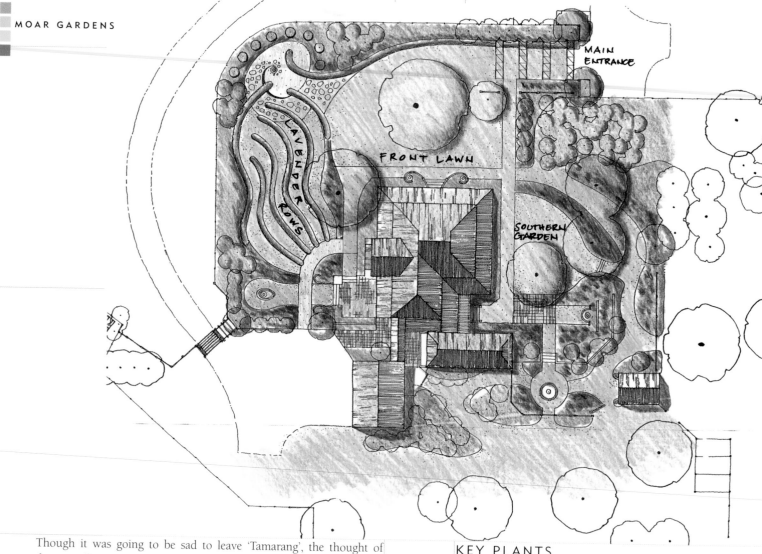

Though it was going to be sad to leave 'Tamarang', the thought of doing it all again was pretty irresistible.

'Campton' was where dad had set his sights. This time 500 acres (200 hectares) of undulating country to the north of Armidale meant dad could become a real farmer. At around five times bigger than 'Tamarang' it meant more grass, more cows, that sort of thing. As for the house, she was a beauty — an eighty-year-old timber farmhouse with a verandah wrapping around the north, south and east. Mum was slightly horrified given the standard of spick and span-ness she had left behind at 'Tamarang' — but she could see the potential.

As for the garden, it was a very typical country garden/old timber farmhouse combo. On the north and east sides of the house the fence was relatively tight, in close to the house. If it were a house and garden in town the proportions and scale would have seemed generous, but when in the middle of vast open space they seemed out of scale with their surrounds. To the west of the house a row of huge cypress (*Cupressus* species) protected the house from the winter westerlies. This windbreak was only metres (a few feet) from the house and towered above the roofline. To the south the garden stretched out and would have been quite spacious had it not been for the tangle of trees clogging it up.

KEY PLANTS

TREES
Acer buergerianum
  (Trident maple)
Betula pendula
  (Silver birch)
Cedrus deodara
  (Himalayan cedar)
Pistacia chinensis
  (Chinese pistachio)

CLASSIC PERENNIALS AND ROSES
Consolida ajacis (Larkspur)
David Austin roses
Delphinium elatum
Digitalis purpurea
  (Foxglove)
Rosa 'Albertine'
Rosa 'Iceberg'
Rosa banksiae

SHRUBS FOR SILVERS/GREYS/PURPLES
Artemisia sp. (Wormwood)
Lavandula intermedia
Salvia 'Indigo Spires'
Santolina chamaecyparissus
  (Cotton lavender)
Teucrium fruticans

TO LAWN OR NOT TO LAWN?

Be aware that in dry countries like Australia the greenest lawns take a lot of work and commitment — constant watering, feeding, weeding and mowing. The long-term plan at 'Campton' is to reduce the lawn size. Even though a drought-tolerant species of grass (a new variety of buffalo) has been used, when the summers are dry and hot it's hard to resist wasting precious water to prevent the lawn from turning brown. In time the lawn area will be reduced by about 30 per cent, replaced by paths of decomposed granite and areas of paving. These will in turn create definite edges to the lawn areas, giving them a more defined shape.

The garden at 'Campton' is roughly divided into four sections that developed in different stages over a period of years. The southern garden (above) is shaded by a *Pistacia chinensis* and bordered by a bed of perennials including foxgloves and delphiniums. Each garden space flows smoothly one into the other, wrapping around the old timber farmhouse (top right). The *Acer buergerianum* (bottom right) takes centre stage in the southern garden.

The garden had great potential, and being able to start with a whole raft of mature trees was priceless.

You wouldn't have described the house as a grand old lady — rather she was a nice old duck whose age was starting to catch up with her. She needn't have worried, however, because the Moars were all charged up ready to breathe new life into her. As with many old homes, the front part of the house retained its lovely original proportions and large simple rooms, while the back had become something of a rabbit warren with an outdated kitchen and bathrooms. Naturally this whole section required the most urgent surgery, and as part of this mum and dad planned on adding a whole new wing that was to become their bedroom.

In designing these improvements, I was particularly mindful of opening up the house to the garden on all sides (with the exception of the west). It already had a good relationship with the north and the east aspect thanks to the verandah wrapping around the house, but as it stood it was closed to the south — which had the most potential, being protected by generous stands of mature trees, notably a beautifully formed *Acer buergerianum* (trident maple).

The architect came up with a solution: to create a new sleeping wing on the southeastern corner of the house that effectively made

the house 'L' shaped. This layout would give new value to the southern garden — now it would seem loved and included.

The renovations took place over three years, and though mum and I were itching to get the garden started there was no point until the house was finished. This breathing space instead gave plenty of time for planning and designing.

Like any garden it was a case of identifying the strengths and weaknesses, then solving the weaknesses and exploiting the strengths. On the broadest level the problem of scale needed to be addressed. Those tight boundaries on the north and south needed to be pushed out so that the house could breathe and the size of the garden was in keeping with the adjacent (vast) space.

It was clear the garden was going to encircle the house and so would be divided into four sections. The first section was to the west at the rear of the house and would remain more or less unchanged — a small orchard with decaying, deserted chook yards and a place where the working dogs could call home.

The second section (and the first section where work would commence) was to the south. Once it had undergone a hard edit to clear out the overabundance of trees growing in it, this section would be a protected garden with a small lawn, sheltered by a mix of old trees and recently planted natives.

The third section to the north would be brand new, with boundaries extended to give the whole house and garden some decent size and breathing space. The key for this section was to find some way of creating a harmonious transition between the garden and the broader landscape. Whatever happened here was going to be the 'X' factor bit.

The fourth and final section at the front of the house was purely about creating a generous lawn, a simple open space that gave full respect to the house — so that you could appreciate the loveliest aspects of the house from within the garden. As it stood, looking back towards the house from within the garden gave a constricted, shortsighted view.

As the garden at 'Campton' has evolved over the last eight or so years it has paralleled my own evolution as a designer and the refining of my own philosophical approach to gardens. Sense of place is what it all comes down to — trying to work out what it is that is special, unique or characteristic about a particular place and finding a way of expressing that in a garden. It sounds simple and complicated all at the same time. The secrets of a place that you are trying to unlock are usually right under your nose, and it's generally a matter of looking at it all with fresh eyes.

For 'Campton', things became a little more contemporary, in line with my evolution in approach as time progressed.

The first section we began work on was the southern garden. This had loads of potential to become a shaded, sheltered haven. Completely protected and enclosed by old conifers and bounded by the old green shed and of course the new 'L' shape of the house, this had a totally different feel and character to the north and east sides of

STEELY SUPPORT

I've never been a fan of timber lattice of the mass-produced variety — within a couple of years it can begin to warp, twist and look very average. Steel reinforcement mesh that is normally used in concrete provides a very solid, simple and elegant support for growing climbing plants. You can leave it untreated and let it rust or have it coated by getting it professionally galvanized. You'll need to look under industrial galvanizers in your phone book. Naturally this takes more effort than your regular timber lattice, but the long-term results are well worth it in my book.

Mum is very particular about the mowing (top left) and won't let anyone else near the lawnmower (I swear!). The old garage marks the south-west corner of the garden. An 'Albertine' climbing rose scrambles over a screen made of steel reinforcement mesh (bottom far left). The verandah (bottom left) looks out over the surrounding landscape and the distant horizon.

the house which were open to adjacent rural landscape. There were two main things to fix here: the tangle of trees and the sloping ground level.

Overplanting a garden with trees is a common mistake, particularly when you're beginning with a blank canvas. This however, hadn't been a blank canvas for at least eighty years; it called for some heavy garden editing, some 'tough love', garden-style. Thankfully there were three trees that were well formed, and once the rest of the trees were removed they were perfectly positioned. Two large *Pistacia chinensis* (Chinese pistachios) with interlocking canopies stood at the edge of the new garden, with the stunning *Acer buergerianum* right in the centre of the space. This beautiful pyramid-shaped tree was begging to be surrounded by nothing but lawn in order to become the specimen tree it so deserved to be. In fact this maple became the most remarked-upon tree in the whole garden.

With the trees cleared it was time to fix the level issue. The ground sloped from the front southeastern corner of the house away to the southwest and felt like it didn't want to be part of the garden. By building up the ground level with a retaining wall, we created a level garden, and in combination with the new 'L' shape to the house and the cleared trees, the garden space now had a firm, integrated relationship with the house.

I'm a real sucker for the romance of cool climate gardens that owe their influence to all things English — roses, larkspurs (*Consolida* species), delphiniums and poppies when grown to perfection and in abundance will soften the hardest of hearts. The southern garden was the place for us to completely indulge in what I regard as a pretty nostalgic, and dare I say it, pretty traditional approach to planting. David Austin roses, philadelphus, agapanthus, buddleias and lavender formed a loose structure. Interplanted through it were delphiniums, larkspurs and campanulas and anything else with blue tones and vertical form. As this garden continues to evolve I'm blown away by its beauty and softness every spring and summer.

For all intents and purposes this is a walled garden, bound by the conifers, the old orchard and the house — and this makes it possible to do almost anything, because it's not being viewed against the broader landscape.

As much as I loved these gardens, I knew that the new sections to the north needed a different approach. Given my own increasing exposure to a wide range of philosophies about garden making and

landscape on a broader level, things needed to be a little more unconventional. The soft European plantings, to my eye, are a jarring, incongruous experience when placed against a backdrop of all things Australian. You can get away with it when the seasons are excellent and the paddocks are at their most verdant green, but as things start to dry off, the olives, golds and browns start to make the imported plantings look totally out of place.

This is where the lavender rows come in. The first reaction to dealing with this dilemma of mismatched garden and broader landscape could have been to simply plant Australian native specimens. But for this garden that would have been too much of a departure, and we'd have lost the thread and flow of the whole garden. A better approach was to find a way of using foliage and flower colour, combined with the shapes and forms of the garden spaces, to make a strong link to the outlying landscape. The lavender rows were an almost perfect solution.

I've long been utterly seduced by the romance of lavender farms and the strong graphic statement that endless rows of purple make on French and Italian hillsides. Arranging them in sinuous curves in the northeast corner of the garden solved all sorts of issues, at the same time injecting a very contemporary flavour into 'Campton'. The lavender rows make a very strong connection with the outlying landscape. Their sinuous layout echoes that of nearby crops and the shapes they make as you move around and through them match the undulations of the surrounding slopes and hills.

Similarly, the lavender rows are oriented so that they propel your eye out to the wider view — they make no attempt to contain your attention within the garden confines, but encourage you to look beyond it. On a colour level, the silver, grey-green and purples of the lavender (*Lavandula* x *intermedia* to be exact) are a perfect match for the (ever-changing) colour palette of the adjacent paddocks.

The most recently completed section at 'Campton' was the large grass area at the front of the house, worked up in conjunction with the lavender rows. Though this is essentially an open area, it is a good example of the balance of negative and positive space and the importance of different-sized areas adjacent to one another.

In this front section three elements were particularly important — the front view of the house, the huge *Cedrus deodara* (Himalayan cedar) smack bang in the middle of the space and the view out to the paddocks beyond.

A pale yellow Banksian rose scrambles over the metal archways that mark the entrance to 'Campton'.

The lavender rows provide a link to the surrounding landscape. All other plants in this area are predominantly silver foliaged — santolina and *Salvia leucantha* (foreground) and *Teucrium fruticans* (top right of main shot). The lavender (*Lavandula* x *intermedia*) is cut back hard every autumn before the onset of the frosty winters.

Nothing could be allowed to compete with any of these elements, so the best thing was to treat each element with the respect it deserved and do as little as possible. The planting combinations of greys, silver and blues found in the teucrium and artemisia used next to the lavender rows were extended along the fence boundary — as was a lavender row that 'fed' into the main pattern of rows.

The trickiest thing to try and incorporate was an entry into the front garden for visitors, giving a grand sense of arrival on special occasions. An obvious thing to do was to line up some type of entry arbour with the axis of the front door. This would have suddenly made the whole place much grander and far more audacious than it ever had been originally — and this was not what 'Campton' was about. I always find this type of symmetry projected out into a natural landscape at total odds — the two elements don't sit comfortably with each other at all.

Similarly, by building an arbour in front of the house we risked detracting from the best aspect of the building, with its verandah and simple roof line. The solution was to tuck the entry around to the side so that you are delivered out onto the lawn at right angles to the house — from here you are free to enjoy the house and the lone (enormous) *Cedrus deodara* unhindered by any other introduced elements.

One of the most interesting things about a garden is seeing how new visitors respond to it. When 'Campton' has been open as part of the open garden scheme, people seem to be happy to absorb the detail of flowers and colour — but invariably it's the lavender and the more adventurous moments of the garden that draw the best responses.

BARBED WIRE BALLS

Finding the right piece of sculpture for a garden that has a connection with you and where your garden is can be a challenge. The barbed wire balls conceived and created by Adam Jones and Hugh Main of Spirit Level Designs were perfect. Barbed wire is a common element used in the paddocks around 'Campton' (and throughout Australia). The simple idea of rolling it into large spheres creates an object that is at once familiar yet sculptural, with a definite contemporary edge and flavour. Unlike classical European statuary which can look oddly out of place in many Australian gardens, the barbed wire balls feel as if they belong.

AN ALPINE GARDEN

The garden needed to match the imposing design of the house (below left). Blue *Festuca glauca* and the strawlike colours of *Poa labillardieri* (right) hug well-positioned granite rocks that double as a set of steps. The water source for this garden appears to be an underground spring that has breached the surface — a believable 'pretend' watercourse. An enormous *Agonis flexuosa* (centre far right) sits contentedly in the corner of the garden shading a calm, shallow pool.

FAITHFUL RE-CREATION

DESIGNED BY DIETER SCHWARTZ AND RICK DAY

FROM A GARDEN THAT STRIVES TO FORGE A LINK WITH THE OUTLYING LANDSCAPE, TO A GARDEN THAT LINKS HOUSE TO EARTH — A GARDEN THAT IS AN EQUAL MATCH FOR AN IMPOSING MODERNIST HOME

The architecture of a house plays a big role in what shape its garden takes. A stock standard approach is to match and replicate through the garden the form and materials that have been established in the building itself. By this reckoning, standing out the front of Hal Walter's Melbourne home, you'd expect the garden to be just as formidable, bold, pared back and angular.

But as you pass through this slick contemporary pad out onto the upper terrace you're in for a bit of a surprise. As you gaze over the railing and survey the scene, you immediately realize the garden that partners Hal's design is a significantly softer creature than you might have expected. For some reason though, the partnering is perfect.

The direction this garden has taken owes much to the alpine landscapes that Hal has regularly trekked among. Landscapes of glacial valleys and soaring, ruggedly handsome, snow-capped mountain ranges. These are powerful, awe-inspiring places, and for Hal these feelings and responses are similarly generated by bold contemporary architecture.

Thus the essence of an alpine landscape, with all its inherent strength and simplicity, was a perfect marriage for the house. Going for the more natural form of garden was an inspired decision, particularly given the result. This natural route, however, can be a trepidatious one.

You see, nature is a very skilled designer — she's been honing her skills for quite some time now — and if we mere mortals are going to try and emulate her work, by crikey it's got to be good. It essentially comes down to skilful fakery — and nobody likes a bad fake.

Dieter Schwartz and Rick Day knew this only too well when Hal gave them the job of creating a convincing, naturally styled garden to earth his home. Rather than try to transplant an alpine landscape in all its detail, they reduced it to its fundamental elements of rock, water and grass.

Now it's the rock and water bit that can get you into trouble when trying to make things look 'natural'. Working

with these materials in the garden can be a bit like working with children or animals — they can steal the show or they can potentially ruin everything.

Here, both rock and water have been skilfully managed, so much so that visitors assume the creek running through the bottom of the garden has been there all along. With naturalistic water treatments, it's the edges that are often the giveaway. Exposed fibreglass or concrete edges don't quite cut the mustard. Here, edges blurred with caps of granite rock laid above and below the waterline, plus layers of pebble and sand built up over a reinforced concrete shell, create an altogether convincing natural watercourse. The water source is just as critical in fooling everyone that humankind had no part whatsoever in this whole venture — this essentially comes down to common sense, the principles of water physics, and a bit of smoke and mirrors thrown in. Hal's creek is fed by a natural underground spring that has breached the rock surface — or so it would seem!

The planting only serves to enhance and complete the quest for natural-looking nature. A simple palette of grassy strappy-leafed things — *Festuca glauca*, *Dietes bicolor* and *Poa labillardieri* — in combination with expanses of *Juniperus conferta*, flow down and through the garden like lava, engulfing the rock as it's encountered along the way.

The placement of the granite boulders has been handled with the same attention to detail as the watercourse. The seemingly simple act of placing rock in the garden is an art all of its own, and anything less than artistic will undermine the pursuance of high-calibre pretend nature. Rocks that have been carelessly plonked around a garden, will always look like rocks carelessly plonked around a garden. By sticking to the iceberg principle, whereby a significant portion of the generously proportioned granite boulders are buried, Dieter has created a scene where you could be forgiven for questioning which came first — the granitic monolith of architecture or the granite outcrop?

All elements in this garden exude strength, including the sculpture by Rudi Jass (left). Granite boulders have been carefully dug into the slope to ensure they look as realistic as possible. The grasses and groundcover, including *Juniperus horizontalis,* spill down the slope, engulfing the rock, while caps of granite laid above and below the waterline create an entirely convincing natural water's edge.

Appearances can be deceiving.
An unlikely-looking clothesline
area creates a focus
and backdrop for the entire
garden space.

GARDEN 3

MOAR GARDEN

A GARDEN DEEP IN THE HEART OF SUBURBIA,
REPACKAGED TO SEDUCE ITS YOUNG OWNERS INTO
LOVING AND USING IT, REVISITING THE UNASSUMING
ELEMENTS OF CLOTHESLINE, LAWN AND PALING FENCE
TO CREATE A PLACE PROUD OF WHERE IT IS

COMMON DENOMINATOR

Whenever I visit another country I'm always keen to unearth what makes gardens unique or special to a particular area. This is something that is often more obvious to a visitor than someone who has lived in a place for a long time. Being Australian, I love asking the question 'What is an Australian garden?' It elicits all sorts of responses. From 'I don't know, never thought about it' to the most impassioned descriptions accompanied by a complex philosophical diatribe. In Australia, as a relatively young nation, the modern world concept of 'garden' has only been kicking around for just over two hundred years. The traditional custodians of Australia on the other hand — the Aboriginal people — after over 40 000 years, have very different ideas about what a garden is, particularly an 'Australian' one.

While I don't think it's that important that we come up with a definitive answer to what an Australian garden is, I think that by asking the question it gets us thinking about a few key things. What is the essence of an Australian garden? What is the feeling of being in a garden in Australia? The quality of light? The sense of space? The relationship both light and space have with our homes? What are the characteristic elements in our gardens? And of course — what's growing in them?

One stereotype that is often put forward as the typical Australian garden is the quarter acre block (that's about 0.1 hectares), complete with surrounding paling fence and a big grassy lawn — big enough of course for a game of cricket on Christmas day. While this type of yard — and all it contains, such as the barbecue and the Hills Hoist — has definitely reached icon status, there has to be room for improvement on this tired old imagery.

But old habits die hard, and it takes time to change things that are the stuff of legends. Scott and Renae were keen to drag their almost classic back yard of grass and paling fence into the twenty-first century, but there were some things they couldn't give up — namely the lawn. Having a lawn these days is almost a modern-day moral dilemma — to lawn, or not to lawn? As successive droughts tighten their grip and give us all a wake-up call, every water-draining garden activity has to be given careful consideration. Surely garden life wasn't meant to be this complicated?

CUES, CLUES, IDEAS, ELEMENTS, INSPIRATION

SUBURBAN ELEGANCE PRIDE IN IDENTITY FRAME THE LAWN HUMBLE
ELEMENTS PALING FENCE AND CLOTHESLINE BEAUTY IS EVERYWHERE
LOVE WHERE YOU LIVE BRING TO LIFE update

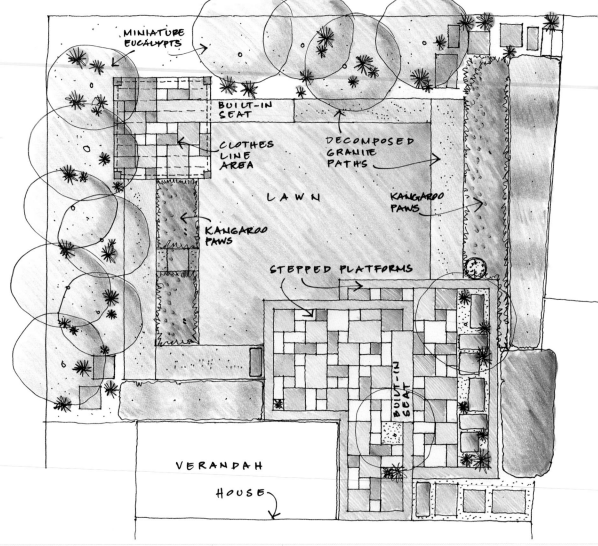

KEY PLANTS

TREES
Eucalyptus 'Summer
   Beauty'
Eucalyptus 'Summer Red'

FEATURE/FLOWERING PLANTING
Actinotus helianthi
   (Flannel flower)
Anigozanthos 'Bushranger'
   (Kangaroo paw)

SHAPEABLE SHRUBS
Westringia fruticans

GRASSES
Festuca glauca
   (Blue fescue)
Miscanthus sinensis
Pennisetum alopecuroides
   'Black Lea'
Poa labillardieri
   (Tussock grass)

It's almost as contentious as my original question 'What is an Australian garden?' The responses are just as impassioned. One thing was for certain — this garden was going to have a lawn in some shape or form.

Scott and Renae had the type of relationship that I find many people have with their garden: a non-relationship. They never used it — never ever. The only time they ventured into it was to dry the washing. Beyond that it was just a space out the back full of grass edged by an inconsequential collection of unloved plants. Scott and Renae certainly weren't proud of this, so they sought counsel in order that owners and garden could be reconciled!

On the plus side this sun-filled garden had a great sense of space to it. After spending a lot of time toiling in small garden spaces no bigger than a large lounge room, to me this garden seemed enormous. The hardwood paling fence that bounded the garden to the south and the west was pretty nice. It was in perfect structural condition (white-ant free) and had a beautiful, weathered, silver patina. It can be pretty easy to lump paling fences in the dull category, but they can be quite handsome and possess real charm. It does help, however, if you have the fence's good side facing into your garden — the palings, as opposed to the posts and rails.

KANGAROO PAWS
Kangaroo paws (*Anigozanthos* and *Macropidia* species) (above right) continue to grow in popularity in Australia and abroad. New colours and improved varieties are constantly being released. In the past, they had a reputation as being difficult to grow due to their susceptibility to ink spot — nasty-looking black splotches covering both leaves and stems. These days, nurseries stock varieties that are much more resilient. To give them the best chance in life make sure they have good drainage and receive at least half a day of full sun. Some breeders recommend that once they have finished flowering in autumn they be cut back to ground level (both flowers and foliage) to encourage fresh new growth in spring.

Plantwise the garden had a nice maturing *Acacia baileyana* to one side. Like most acacias, this is a short-lived tree (this particular species is even regarded as a weed in some areas), but it still gave some clues to the direction of the new planting. So too did the view over the back fence. A majestic eucalypt stood in the neighbours' yard — I really liked the view that took in the 'silver' fence, the shed (to the north of the garden, creating the third boundary) and the neighbours' grand eucalypt — it was an evocative Australian image, and something to take advantage of.

On the down side, there was a certain contraption hogging pole position in the garden — a structure so iconic that to talk disparagingly of it could be viewed as un-Australian. I refer, of course, to the Hills Hoist. I have no issue whatsoever with drying clothes out in the elements — solar any day! But I can never work out why clothes hoists — which, let's face it, are totally aesthetically challenged — always get to have the best position in the garden. Again, if we're being honest, they never 'add' to a garden space, they always detract. While the clothes hoists you can remove and store out of sight are a fine idea, how many times do you really move them? Invariably they stay put forever. There had to be some means of drying the clothes in the garden that didn't compromise the space.

The main issue in this garden was getting people out of the house and keeping them there. Platforms lure people off the back verandah and down into the garden. The lawn was retained and 'honoured', remaining more or less square in shape and framed by paths of decomposed granite.

The palette of materials was a response to the weathered silver timbers of the old paling fence. The combination of rendered brick seats and grey concrete pavers ensures the fence remains an important part of the scheme. Colour comes via mass-planted kangaroo paws.

The other main thing that was holding this garden back — stunting the potential relationship between Scott and Renae and their garden — was the connection from house to garden. As it stood, you walked from the kitchen through sliding doors onto a covered deck and . . . stayed there. From there you generally returned to the kitchen and reclaimed your position at the breakfast bar. The problem was that the deck was surrounded by lattice and an overgrown wisteria that more or less caged you in. This quickly diffused any intentions you may have had of exploring the back yard. Added to this, the deck was a good metre (just over 3 feet) above the ground level of the garden. If there's one thing that puts up a little psychological barrier about venturing from house to garden it's a level change of more than a couple of steps.

So which way forward? Beyond solving the functional problems of this garden it was important to pinpoint what was special about this place and the locale and use that as the inspiration for creating the 'flavour' of this garden. The home is deep in the heartland of suburban Sydney, an area that proliferated post war — particularly through the 1960s. This is classic quarter acre block territory and you could be forgiven for thinking that there's little to draw inspiration from. It's a place low on distinctive architecture, landmarks and natural features. But there is always a way of turning what seems to be a negative into a positive.

There is I believe an inherent elegance to the simplicity of the quarter acre block, the paling fences, carpets of lawn and all that goes along with it. With this garden it was a matter of getting back to the simplicity of these essential elements and making something of them. Rather than trying to transport the visitor to some distant land by recreating Morocco or Tuscany in western Sydney, it was a case of creating a simple space, true to its suburban roots, while giving it a distinctive Australian flavour. I want whoever is in the garden to be happily aware of where they are — and to be proud of it.

WEATHERED TIMBER AND METAL

Reusing secondhand timber makes sense environmentally and aesthetically, and the patina of weathered hardwood can be irresistible. Weathered hardwood responds well to being rubbed back with a wire brush, rather than being replaned or resanded: brushing preserves the silver colour of the wood and other characteristics that give it its unique look and feel. Weathered hardwood contrasted with silver metals such as aluminium and stainless steel lends an effect of softness and warmth to these otherwise cold, hard-edged materials. Conversely, using silver metals with weathered timber can bring a welcome contemporary edge to a structure. Just because it's secondhand don't expect it to be cheap — the price of secondhand hardwood is generally the same as new.

CONCRETE PAVERS

There is a plethora of paving materials available on the market these days and the choice is anything but simple. In your pursuit of the perfect paver don't overlook the humble concrete paver — the type commonly available from your nursery or hardware store. They're inexpensive and when laid well they make a simple, neutral ground surface that doesn't overpower or compete with other elements in the garden. If plain grey is too dull for you, try mixing it up with darker shades or colouring the pavers with coloured concrete washes available from specialist paint stores.

The key really was the lawn. If we were going to keep it, it was about giving it some shape and purpose — making it the central heart of the garden. Then it was a matter of breaking through the barriers around the deck attached to the house and creating a free flow of space and movement from the house to the lawn.

The shape of the lawn could have been anything — freeform amoebic edges or geometric curves and circles — but to remain true to those suburban lawn origins, I thought it best to keep things simple and rectangular. The next thing to consider was its size. Big lawns mean more water, so reducing the size of the lawn effectively reduces the amount of watering. The size and shape of the lawn then set up the geometry for the whole garden. Keeping the lawn small meant there was room to further enhance its shape and presence by framing it with paths of decomposed granite and planting beds.

The next step was to encourage and entice people out of the house and into the garden. The solution was to play with the two top activities slated for this garden — entertaining and clothes drying. The entertaining side of things provided the opportunity to develop a series of platforms that slowly led down from the existing deck. Big generous platforms that gently enticed people down into the garden, removing that psychological barrier of level change as well as providing a paved

space up against the lawn. A built-in seat incorporated into the platforms meant there was somewhere to sit — a sneaky little trick to keep people out in the garden rather than turning on their heels and heading back to the breakfast table!

Believe it or not, the need to maintain somewhere to dry clothes was the exciting bit of the design. I've always wondered why more people don't design clotheslines that look nothing like clotheslines, that somehow add to the garden's aesthetics. Pergolas are perfect. The only thing you need to take into account is the height. Whoever is the shortest clothes-hanger-outer-er needs to determine the structure's height. Putting the clothesline/pergola to the rear corner of the garden meant you had to pass through the entire garden to get to it, another sneaky way of ensuring that you interact with the garden.

The aluminium top with large-sectioned reused hardwood timber posts makes for a very smart structure. The timber is earthy and 'grounded', while the aluminium top gives the structure a nice contemporary edge. The backdrop to the structure — the random criss-cross of stainless steel cables — serves as a much-needed focal point for the entire space.

Beyond the overall layout and structure of this garden the Australian 'flavour' comes via the planting scheme and the palette of

The circular pots (far left) containing flannel flowers create an effective contrast against the squares and rectangles of the seat and pavers. The kangaroo paws (*Anigozanthos* 'Bushranger') (top and above) bring a distinctive Australian flavour to the garden.

105

With a simple planting scheme, including kangaroo paws (far left) and an uncomplicated palette of hard materials (left), the garden has an unmistakable sense of identity.

MOAR GARDEN 3

materials. Reused hardwood timber, decomposed granite and sandstone create a very earthy combination that has a sense of age and history to it. The contrasting use of aluminium, stainless steel and simple concrete pavers, however, ensures that the garden maintains a crisp modern edge.

In the end it is always the plants that are going to set the mood and feel of the garden, and for any garden that is trying to capture a true sense of Australia there have to be native plants involved in there somewhere.

I'm certainly no purist when it comes to using Australian natives, but I have great admiration for those who possess the depth of knowledge required to ensure the species used are native to a specific area. I approach it in a more stylized sense, using natives that possess great design qualities or that I strongly identify as being Australian. In this respect I'm always a sucker for kangaroo paws (*Anigozanthos* species). I regard them as the 'rose' of Australia. They are complete scene stealers and have a primitive look to them, capturing the bizarre quality of much Australian flora.

Scott and Renae's garden was a great opportunity to use them en masse, planting them in two rectangular beds flanking the lawn. While there is a huge range of kangaroo paws available these days, I can't really go past the giant reds and yellows. Their flower is clean and simple and the flowerheads themselves can reach up to 1.5 metres (5 feet).

To maintain a simple planting scheme and keep it clearly Australian, the edges of the garden have been planted with a small 'forest' of miniature eucalypts. These have only been available for the last few years and their popularity is steadily increasing. They only reach around 5 metres (16 feet) in height and flower prolifically in red, orange or pink. At the base of the trees a mix of grasses has been planted, including *Festuca glauca*, *Pennisetum alopecuroides* (the black one), *Poa poiformis* 'Kingsdale' and *Miscanthus sinensis*. These are then mulched with a layer of white pebble (crushed quartz). It's almost a Japanese approach to planting. The intention is to give enough air and space around each grass so you can fully appreciate its form and habit. The carpet of quartz as mulch is intended to further enhance the grasses by creating a clean, pure background to view them against. At no point are the grasses and eucalypts meant to mask the paling fence — it's as much a part of the composition as anything else.

Scott and Renae's suburban garden was a great opportunity to explore the whole idea of finding inspiration in the most unlikely of places. Drawing on the most unassuming of elements has created a garden that makes a confident statement about where it is, while at the same time encouraging Scott and Renae to truly engage with their outdoor space.

A TRADITIONAL GARDEN

Gardening keeps you young — Jean prunes a crab apple (*Malus* sp.) (right). Behind her (right of shot) is a fifty-year-old mock orange (*Philadelphus* sp.) planted by her father. This garden is a place where good old-fashioned work reaps great rewards (far right): an abundant supply of vegetables and an ever-changing parade of flowers throughout spring, autumn and summer.

QUIETLY ROMANTIC

DESIGNED BY JEAN WAUGH

FROM THE CONTEMPORARY REPACKAGING OF AN AUSTRALIAN SUBURBAN GARDEN, TO THE QUIET ROMANCE OF A MORE TRADITIONAL APPROACH

Jean Waugh's garden is a garden of memories. It takes me back to my childhood, which is quite odd, because our garden was nothing like Jean's. It's a safe familiar place, which is also quite odd since it reminds me of the garden I'd walk past on the way to primary school where I'd pick the flowers poking through the front fence — only to be yelled at by the scary lady who lived inside. Most of all though, it reminds me why I love gardens.

Jean's garden is an exuberant, ramshackle, much-loved patch of earth. It's a quiet testament to the simple act of gardening. Without any pretence or self-conscious design, this garden captures what is at the heart of garden making and garden keeping — the joy of planting things and seeing what happens.

Somehow I've managed to earn a reputation as a flower hater. Just because I design a few gardens that rely on things other than flowers I get lumbered with this horrible title. It's on a par with being mean to puppies and babies. For the record, I love flowers and puppies and babies! It's just that in pursuing the brave new world of gardening it's easy to be perceived as anti-tradition. This couldn't be further from the truth. Sure I'm keen to forge new garden frontiers, but I'm a total sucker for a border of roses and delphiniums.

Even if you weren't a pushover for a bit of floral profusion, a garden as quietly romantic as Jean's has to soften even the hardest modernist, minimalist, clean-edged heart.

Sizewise Jean Waugh is just under 1.5 metres tall (a compact 4 feet 11 inches). Agewise? Let's just say Jean is well and truly past scoring her half-century, but upon meeting her you quickly realize this is completely irrelevant. Moving a cubic metre (close to 1½ cubic yards) of sand or removing the odd apple tree here or there isn't given a second thought. Not really a problem for someone who looks like grandmother material but confides she's got a homemade catapult ready to go just in case the local revheads speeding up and down the side lane need to be shown who's boss.

For Jean, descended from a long line of diligent gardeners, hard work is nothing new or foreign. Her father, for example, would get up at the obscenely early hour of 3 a.m. in order to beat the heat of the day to keep the neighbourhood stocked with a full range of fresh fruit and veggies. In 1983 Jean took over the garden from her dad. With no real intention of keeping it exactly as her father had, nor with visions of making sweeping changes, Jean simply carried on gardening. Changes took place as they naturally needed to — and mostly for practical reasons. Two apple trees producing too much fruit were removed (by Jean of course). Similarly a couple of ornamental flowering peaches whose low-lying limbs were hindering lawn mowing were shown the back gate.

The additions, however, have far outweighed the subtractions. Over the years Jean has gradually added garden beds, doing away with most of the lawn, stuffing them full of cold-climate perennials — including the red roses and blue delphiniums that Jean's stepmother Edna had had great success in growing. In more recent years the veggie patch has been resurrected and has resumed its rightful back corner garden position.

Jean well and truly subscribes to the cottage garden philosophy — perennial favourites like columbines (*Aquilegia* species), valerian and geums self-seed freely through the garden, popping up wherever they feel like it, turning on the colour and movement.

There is a sense of homecoming when you visit this garden, a sensation that gardens (and homes) that have been scraped back to a blank slate can't quite re-create. The missing component is time. With time comes the layers of stories and telltale signs that years of interaction with people and nature leave on a garden. This is what gives a garden soul — and when gardens have it, you want to return to them time after time.

While this is a garden that highlights how far contemporary garden design has come, it's a grounding reminder of what it sometimes forgets. At no point do I think we should abandon contemporary thinking in favour of good old-fashioned gardening values, but there's no reason why the essence of traditional gardening — that simple passion of growing and tending — cannot be part of modern garden making.

Opium poppies (*Papaver somniferum*) reach for the sun against a backdrop of spiraea, red valerian (*Centranthus ruber*) and a Virginia creeper (*Parthenocissus* sp.) scrambling up the old garage (left). The garden is overflowing with spring-flowering roses (top right), opium poppies (upper right), Californian poppies (*Eschscholzia* sp.) (lower right), and more opium poppies (bottom right)!

All structures in this garden were built from reclaimed timbers and secondhand metal products. Though the garden is small it is delineated into distinct zones, with the vegetable patch (foreground) the star of the garden.

MOAR GARDEN 4

A GARDEN INVERTED, WITH THE NORMALLY OUT-OF-SIGHT TASK OF GROWING VEGETABLES CONFIDENTLY AND IRREVERENTLY SERVED UP ONTO CENTRE STAGE, INSPIRED BY THE MOST UNLIKELY OF ELEMENTS, SOURCED FROM THE MOST UNLIKELY OF PLACES

VEGETABLE CENTRAL

Veggie patches are like pets. They seem like a great idea at the time, but once the romance and novelty wear off, the reality of the work sets in. Suddenly, they're all about commitment and dedication. While I may have made the classic well-intended gift faux pas of giving an irresistibly cute kitten to a friend for Christmas, I've never made the mistake of forcing a veggie patch onto someone who didn't want it.

Fortunately Emma McDonald was a dedicated gardener, a long-time gardening convert who had a genuine passion for tending plants — a prerequisite for anyone about to take on their first vegetable patch. For me, the added advantage was that Emma was up for anything — the crazier the better. Emma was also keen for her two boys to take on responsibility for the garden, and a veggie patch seemed as good a way as any to achieve this.

As it stood, the garden was pretty regular, straight up and down, short back and sides. With its bog standard ground-level garden beds surrounding a sea of extremely brown (ugly) brick paving, the garden's saving grace was Emma's additions, notably her much-loved bright red outdoor dining table. For me the table — or more accurately its vibrant colour — was a nice little indicator of her penchant for the quirkier side of things.

The garden seemed small. However, this is something that I've come to learn is all relative. The yard measured around 10 x 5 metres (33 x 16 feet). If they were the dimensions of an interior room, it would be enormous. But much of these 50 square metres (538 square feet) of garden were already occupied, seriously compromising the useable space for people. The unfortunate thing was that the compromiser in question was a beautifully formed Japanese maple (*Acer palmatum*). These trees are slow growers at the best of times, and it was not yet tall enough for us to effectively lift its canopy to create a useful shade-giving tree. It was a case of beautiful tree, wrong shape, wrong height and wrong spot. You would normally make concessions for such a lovely tree and design around it, but this time it had to shift — to somewhere else in the garden hopefully.

Meanwhile the 'doing' list in Emma's garden was increasing: a place to dine, entertain, relax, garden and feed the family. In a space measuring a tight 10 x 5 metres (33 x 16 feet), could it all fit? Of course

CUES, CLUES, IDEAS, ELEMENTS, INSPIRATION
HARVEST ONE PERSON'S TRASH ANOTHER PERSON'S TREASURE
MIRROR MIRROR REINTERPRET DIG ROW UPON ROW FEAST
CHEEKY IN THE SPOTLIGHT GRAPHIC ELEMENTS

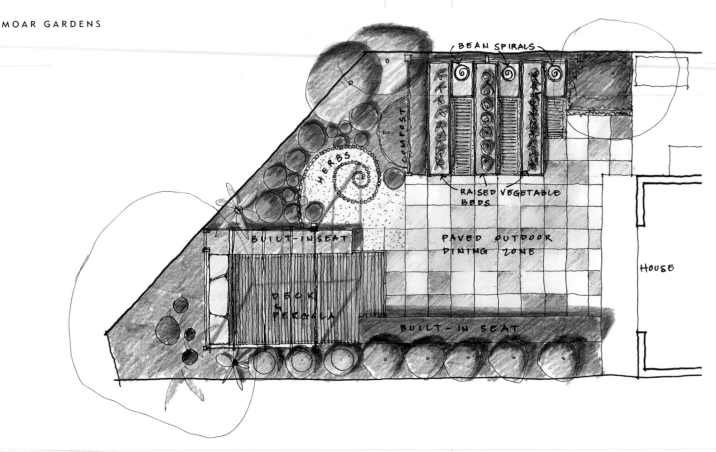

KEY PLANTS

SHRUBS

Buxus microphylla
   (Japanese box)
Camellia sasanqua
Liriope muscari 'Evergreen
   Giant'
Murraya paniculata
   (Orange jessamine)

VARIOUS VEGGIES AND
HERBS

Rosemary
Coriander
Basil
Thyme
Oregano
Chives
Beans
Tomatoes
Rhubarb
Carrots
Spring onions
Rainbow chard

it could! Small spaces only start to become interesting when the pressure's on!

Making the decision about what we want to do in the garden leads to the next inevitable stage — what shape and form is it all going to take? Having only just recently discovered the brilliant and irreverent garden designer Diarmuid Gavin from the UK, I was completely inspired by his jaw-dropping designs. A quick review of his work is enough to make anyone feel uptight and conservative by comparison, and I took it as a sign to cut loose.

A veggie patch was always going to be at the heart of this garden, but now I had all the motivation I needed to take it to the next level. Invariably veggie patches have had a utilitarian, back of the yard, out of sight position in the garden hierarchy — hard working, but not altogether beautiful. This was a chance to bring it centre stage and exploit all the design possibilities that the tradition of growing vegetables provides.

The regimented rows that vegetables are traditionally grown in are by their very nature visually graphic and perfect for incorporating into a contemporary geometric scheme. This really is no secret; the French were onto it a long time before me with their elegant potagers and kitchen gardens laid out with intricate precision.

Raised rows of veggies became the central focus of the space. No trumped-up pond masquerading as a water feature to steal the show — here it was going to be all about the veggies. To organize the garden spatially, I divided it into four clear but interlocking zones. The main paved area had built-in seating running down its edge, backed by a

Liriope (right) 'explodes' out of the top of planters constructed from sheets of miniature corrugated iron. Succulents adorn the paling fence (top far right) and heavy metal drainage grates set into quartz gravel (bottom far right) make very practical, handsome paths running between the raised vegetable planters.

SCRAP METAL DISCOVERIES

Sourcing secondhand furniture and timber is a relatively straightforward pursuit, but tracking down scrap metal can require a bit more gumption. Scrap metal yards are where you'll find the interesting, useful and unusual metal items — the only thing is the scrap metal merchant is generally more interested in getting them melted down to build the next round of 747s than in selling them to a garden creator with quirky ideas. This is where you need to muster all your confidence and charm to persuade them to let you fossick. The easier route is to take a long, studious walk around your hardware store, where you'll find many things that can double as interesting plant containers. Just make sure they're made of durable materials like galvanized metals or PVC (polyvinyl chloride), and that you can create adequate drainage holes in them.

small deck and pergola. To the side of that was the herb area, and taking centre stage next to the new paving was the veggie patch.

At no point were we trying to pretend that this was a veggie patch that was going to keep the family going week in week out. Quite the opposite — this was purely a chance to 'have a go'. There are several factors to take into account when growing veggies. Firstly, the amount of sun: you need at least five hours of full sun per day. Next, but equally as important, are excellent drainage and organic, healthy soil. While you can give the latter two a helping hand, you can't add extra sunlight — if you ain't got the light, say good night!

The challenge was to give this veggie patch a modern edge and make it worthy of being at centre stage. This is a lot easier than it sounds. Veggie gardens are highly functional creatures, crammed with elements such as plant supports, raised beds, paths and bird repellers: all things just waiting to be reinvented and reinterpreted (just like the chair!). It's about taking the most familiar and functional of elements and putting a spin on them.

Emma is a collector of street finds and quirky bits and pieces. So it was with total confidence that I suggested this garden be pulled together with pieces unearthed from wherever we could find them: the street, the tip, scrap metal yards, secondhand building centres, auction houses, you name it. To be honest most of this was budget driven, but as they say, necessity is the mother of all invention.

This garden was a great example of how you start with an idea or concept and from there it's shaped and steered by what you find to put into it. I set out with thoughts of timber or metal containers — timber

Reclaimed hardwood timbers enclose the raised vegetable beds (right). The signature spiral (top far right) in the herb section helps retain the gravel. Planters (centre far right) are a mix of found objects and containers specially made from rolls of galvanized sheet metal. The bright red outdoor dining table and purple cement-rendered brick seat (bottom far right) introduce some bold colour.

for the veggie rows (think narrow coffins without a lid) and metal for things like herbs and beans.

The time I spent scrounging through a couple of scrap metal yards proved to be the formative moments for this garden. When recycling like this, you really have to have an open mind, and be prepared to do some serious lateral thinking. Mind you, it can be a frustrating and mind-numbingly-boring experience for anyone accompanying you on your search, which involves long stretches of meditation upon apparently useless articles (as you try to unlock their potential and imagine what they could be — or be part of).

The pile of detritus that gathered as the search dragged on included a tangle of extruded aluminium, four lengths of scaffolding, a huge industrial roll of galvanized sheeting, random lengths and diameters of copper pipe, various old oversized metal cooking pots, half a dozen heavy cast iron drainage grates and a half-round of corrugated iron. A successful haul, and a garden more or less formed on the go.

So what was in store for this bounty of refuse? The scaffolding was destined for the top of a pergola to support a shade-giving ornamental grape vine over the small deck at the back of the space. The extruded aluminium was rolled around a length of 200 millimetre (8 inch) diameter PVC (polyvinyl chloride) drainage pipe to create some very funky bean supports. These were subsequently attached to long galvanized metal exhaust flues — quite the sculptural crowning glory for the whole garden. The copper pipe was to be fixed horizontally between timber posts as support for passion fruit and other climbing plants. The huge roll of galvanized sheeting was cut up and used to construct a range of different-sized planters: some housed camellias, while others served as the key containers for the herb section, and for the relocated Japanese maple. The cast iron grates were laid end to

VEGGIE NECESSITIES

Before you start salivating at the thought of tomatoes that actually taste like tomatoes, you need to ensure you have adequate sun. To grow vegetables successfully you need a bare minimum of five to six hours of full sun per day. The next most important thing is soil and drainage. Your soil needs to be well drained and rich in nutrients and organic matter. If, like the majority of people, you have garden soil that is anything but rich and well drained, you can create built-up garden beds with a minimum depth of 30 centimetres (about a foot), either freeform or with some type of edging retaining the soil. Lack of space should be no deterrent to having a vegetable patch: pots are perfectly fine for growing veggies.

We needed something interesting and unusual for the bean supports. A tangle of extruded aluminium was wound around a PVC pipe to create the bean spirals. There is a nice contrast of opposites in this garden — the outlandish use of mirrors and quirky bean supports and the red painted (dead) tree versus the very grounded pursuit of vegetable growing.

end, inlaid into white quartz gravel between the raised veggie beds, creating a very practical and seriously spunky walking surface. The half-round of corrugated iron was given a marine ply back and lid and became the most essential of veggie patch components — the compost bin. The assortment of old pots and saucepans became character-adding planters for the herb garden.

Beyond all the reclaimed bits and pieces, the one single thing that set this garden apart from your regular urban veggie patch was the decision to use mirrors — lots of them. This is the bit that I can thank Diarmuid Gavin for. Not that I'm suggesting this was a copy of something he did — rather, he provided all the encouragement with his approach and attitude to design, thinking a long way beyond the square. Mirror tiles lining the two boundaries to the veggie section serve to make the space on the whole look bigger. The mirrors also make the actual veggie patch itself look four times bigger than it really is.

This is not a new concept when applied indoors, but suggest using mirrors outside in the garden and people tend to get nervous. Emma was quite concerned about coming face to face with her reflection in the garden every morning. To tone down this whole issue I positioned the salvaged copper pipe in front of the mirrors as a support for climbing plants: these would partially conceal the mirrors, but would still allow enough reflection to give the illusion of a bigger space.

Despite our best efforts, our beloved maple didn't quite make it. This garden was built in January — a blisteringly hot January — and to be honest I never held out great hopes for our little tree. We did all the right things; the only thing was we should have done them in winter. Deciduous trees can generally be moved extremely successfully — but don't rush things, wait for autumn or winter before attempting to transplant them.

So as the maple, which had been transplanted into one of the large containers made from the roll of galvanized sheet metal, slowly turned up its toes, we had to think about how to deal with this unfortunate woody corpse. If in doubt, paint it I say. And that is exactly what Emma did. I suggested she paint it red to match her table and she loved the idea, and now it creates a great entry into what has to be the coolest veggie patch in Bondi.

MIRROR IMAGE
Mirrors can work to great effect in the garden, creating a sense of space as well as adding a major novelty factor. Key considerations are where they are to be placed and what view they're reflecting. It might sound obvious, but in terms of their placement it's crucial to consider what they are reflecting because that is what you end up looking at — you want to see twice the beauty not twice the ugliness. Also consider their orientation towards the sun. Mirrors that reflect the sun can be blinding affairs.

A COUNTRY GARDEN

Old-fashioned red valerian (*Centranthus ruber*) appears throughout the planting (below left). Space flows effortlessly through this garden (right) and planting beds subtly hug the landform contours, making the beds appear as natural as possible. Though full of flowers the planting scheme still has simplicity and strength, thanks to a restrained palette of plants: simple drifts of yellow buttercups (*Ranunculus* sp.), blue forget-me-nots (*Myosotis* sp.) and red valerian. The brick-paved terrace (bottom far right) provides a view over the garden.

FRESH PERSPECTIVE

DESIGNED BY SUSIE MUNRO ROSS

FROM MAKING SENSE OF A SHORTAGE OF SPACE, TO
MAKING SENSE OF AN ABUNDANCE OF SPACE

A big country garden is a very desirable thing, but for all their beauty, these gardens can be difficult beasts and are definitely not without their challenges.

Apart from issues of water supply and, generally speaking, tough growing conditions, there are two things, in design terms, that are the real test for big Australian country gardens. Firstly is how the garden — and house — sit within, and connect with, the area that surrounds them. And secondly, what the hell do you do with all that space?

Opportunities were the things Susie Munro Ross focused on when she first set eyes on this place: 20 hectares (50 acres) of gravelly bush, with an uninspired narrow timber house perched uneasily 1.8 metres (6 feet) above the ground at one end. Ever positive, Susie put her design know-how to the test and set about carving out a garden that embraced the house, making it feel loved and included, blurring the edges between the garden and the wider landscape, and bringing the garden to life by knowing exactly what to do with all that space.

Garden design has become Susie's passion, both professionally and personally, and as an avid disciple of legendary garden designer Russell Page she's honed a very solid understanding of the fundamental design principles of scale, proportion and balance.

One of the key things that attracted Susie to this place was the lie of the land. Most folk's ideal would be a house atop a hill with views. Instead, Susie, like her mentor Mr Page before her, preferred the reverse — a hollow. From the house, the ground rises away from you, so you look into the garden. In a hollow the garden becomes the important view — from a hilltop the garden is secondary as you look out across the top of it with the wider view and landscape stealing your focus.

The first task was to edit the eclectic mix of Australian native and exotic trees that had previously been planted on the site, keeping those that added something and removing those that detracted. Then came the clincher, rectifying that poor union between house and garden. Essentially it was a simple process of constructing retaining walls at the low end of the slope where the house teetered above the ground. Building up the ground level in front of the house made a dramatic change, and suddenly the house looked like it was meant to be there all along.

Using the wide proportions of the house, Susie was then able to extend the verandah: she built a brick-paved terrace, creating a grandly dimensioned outdoor living space that in turn made the house seem even more grounded.

Sticking to a palette of earthy and recycled materials — timber, brick, stone and concrete — mostly unearthed on site, Susie ensured that the garden maintained a distinctive uncontrived country feel.

Beyond the house and terrace, Susie worked in broad brushstrokes to create the wider garden, being ever mindful of the overall composition of spaces that make up the garden. The result is a great example of how your passage through a garden can be manipulated (unbeknown to you of course). The simple freestanding wall — which is also the retaining wall rectifying the initial slope issue — with a concrete ball denoting one end, coaxes and guides you into the garden, giving you the best entry experience the garden has on offer. And it's a lovely one.

This is primarily a garden of trees and spaces. Garden beds are there but are never forced onto the garden — instead they wrap and hug the contours in a fashion you might expect had they occurred naturally. The planting itself is simple and bold, with generous drifts of one plant blending into another — the opposite, almost, of the riot and tumble of cottage garden schemes. There is a subtle play of verticals and horizontals in the planting — the vertical lines of the pink-flowering valerian for example, juxtaposed with the prostrate ramble of buttercups — maintaining great tension and contrast in the scheme. This keeps your eye stimulated and moving around well-composed 'plant pictures'.

A circular pond, a bold geometric element, placed off-centre, reinforces the asymmetry of the garden's layout, and acts as a central point of focus for the whole garden. It's an element you're always drawn back to, from wherever you are in the garden, either physically or visually.

The only place that adheres to a rigid geometry is the side garden adjacent to the house. An abundant herb garden with zigzagging gravel paths dissecting it serves to lengthen and broaden an otherwise thin enclosed space.

For me, this garden stands out from the crowd of Aussie country gardens. Seldom are the principles of scale and proportion so well handled in conjunction with an artistically controlled palette of materials and planting. In this big, beautiful country garden a subtle mix of traditional flavours is carried off with confident contemporary flair.

The power of focus (left and centre right). A simple concrete ball sitting on the end of the low retaining wall creates an attention-grabbing focal point and denotes the entrance to the garden. The zigzag path of the side herb garden (top right) is the only formal geometry used within the garden. The circular pond is an element that your eye is always drawn to no matter where you are in the garden (bottom right).

Each element in this garden was intended to possess its own sculptural identity. The cement-rendered snake seat is one of the most distinctive elements in the garden.

GARDEN 5

A GARDEN CARED FOR AND LOVED, REINVENTED AND REJUVENATED, TO BECOME A PLACE OF SCULPTURAL ELEMENTS, SUBLIME AND BEAUTIFUL — TAKING DESIGN CUES FOR PLANTS AND ARCHITECTURAL FEATURES FROM THE SURROUNDING STREETS

MOAR GARDEN

REINVENTED

One of the biggest challenges you can face in designing gardens is working with an existing garden that is loved and tended. Often it's simpler to take things back to the beginning — a clean slate — and begin again. But when someone has put in hard work mixed with heart and soul it can become difficult to suggest ways forward that don't offend or that offer enough respect to all that has happened before.

Michele and Jeff had mixed feelings about their garden. They loved it but knew there had to be something more they could do with it. Both had enthusiasm and gumption in bucketloads, but just needed a helping hand to get their garden to the next level.

Their house was in suburban southern Sydney, surrounded by solid brick homes built from the 1930s through to the 50s and 60s. These included a mix of Californian bungalows, some of those great ocean liner inspired homes of the 1930s, and some of the more questionable recently built mega mansions which are a testament to many things, the least of them being half decent taste.

Like most people they were making the best of an inherited garden — a place where some decisions and actions in the past were good and great assets to the space, and some were not so brilliant and in an ideal world would be fixed, altered or re-jigged.

I found this a tricky garden to work on. While it was simple enough to identify the garden's strengths and weaknesses, it took a long time to work out what direction to take the design in. The garden was quite large and overall the block of land was triangular in shape. Divided into three sections, some areas were more successful than others. Walking out of the house through french doors (a good start) you stepped out onto a generous-sized timber deck — this was where all the action in this garden took place. From here on, it was a piecemeal affair, with some standout problems.

The key one was the Great Wall of Lattice that ran through the middle of the garden, effectively severing it in two. Stepping off the deck — a drop of about 60 centimetres (2 feet) — onto a paved area, you then walked through a doorway in the looming lattice into the back section of the garden. Here you encountered a water feature installed by Michele and Jeff — built with the best of intentions of luring people down to the far reaches of the garden, but not quite

CUES, CLUES, IDEAS, ELEMENTS, INSPIRATION

SUBLIME REBORN SCULPTURAL UNEXPECTED YET FAMILIAR

REWORK RUST AND STONE TEXTURAL

MAGICAL SPIRAL MANY LEVELS POWER OF THE GRID

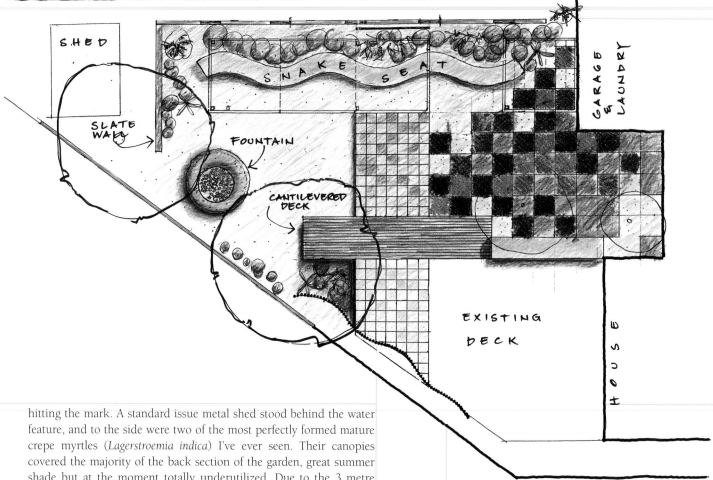

SHED

SLATE WALL

FOUNTAIN

SNAKE SEAT

CANTILEVERED DECK

GARAGE & LAUNDRY

EXISTING DECK

HOUSE

hitting the mark. A standard issue metal shed stood behind the water feature, and to the side were two of the most perfectly formed mature crepe myrtles (*Lagerstroemia indica*) I've ever seen. Their canopies covered the majority of the back section of the garden, great summer shade but at the moment totally underutilized. Due to the 3 metre (10 feet) high lattice screens blocking the back section of the garden, you weren't really aware that the trees were there — which is saying something as these were big trees.

Beyond the lattice issue the other main factor affecting this space was the boundaries of the garden. The garage/laundry was open-sided and not doing us any favours — the inner workings of garages and laundries do not make stunning garden backdrops. An even bigger issue was the boundary to the rest of the garden. A metal fence screened with a row of tightly spaced standardized conifers 3–4 metres (10–13 feet) high flanked either side of the space. Whoever tries to convince you that metal fences (of the mass-produced variety) are smart and appealing probably own shares in the company. Economical, functional and 100 per cent termite-resistant, yes; charming, no.

Taking a walk around the neighbourhood I tried to see what made this area tick, if there was something to pick up on, some element — architectural, natural or even cultural — to possibly exploit for the garden. In this case it was something architectural — metal balustrades. A common feature of a lot of post-war homes of the 1950s and 60s, albeit pretty low key, is the metal balustrades and hand railings used at the entries, beside stairways and supporting verandah and patio roofs. It's simple, unpretentious metalwork, with a beautiful

KEY PLANTS

TREES
Lagerstroemia indica
   (Crepe myrtle)

FEATURE PLANTINGS
Alpinia caerulea 'Redback'
   (Native ginger)
Drepanostachyum falcatum (Himalayan weeping bamboo)

GRASSES/VERTICAL FORM
Dietes grandiflora
Dietes iridioides
Juncus effusus (Rush)
Lomandra longifolia 'Tanika'
Ophiopogon variegatus
   (Variegated mondo grass)

SHAPEABLE SHRUBS
Buxus microphylla
   (Japanese box)

SUCCULENTS FOR PATCHWORK
Echeveria sp.
Graptopetalum paraguayense
   (Mother-of-pearl plant)
Sempervivum sp.

ALUMINIUM

Aluminium is often overlooked as a material for garden structures, people generally opting for steel or timber. Many of the structures featured in this book have aluminium incorporated in their construction. For non-load-bearing structures, rectangular hollow sections of aluminium can span greater distances than can timber with similar cross-sectional areas. The aluminium structures in this book were constructed at a sheet metal fabricating workshop and then manually lifted into position on site. If these components had been made of steel a crane would have been needed. Aluminium has a beautiful, soft, even grey lustre, which acts as a nice highlight and contrast against darker colours and plant foliage.

The snake seat acts as a 'spine' for the space, stitching the top and bottom levels together (top left). The rust walls sit in front of the true property boundary, concealing the metal fence and the unattractive trunks of the conifers. A patchwork grid of pavers and succulents (top right) contrasts against the curving lines of the snake seat.

fineness of line and a standard stock of shapes and designs including rectangles, diamonds and circles. The one that is possibly the most iconic is the spiral. For me, this shape has perennial appeal, and I thought it would be perfect put to use in the garden somehow.

The owners had certainly thrown up the challenge to me when they said they wanted to take this garden to the 'next level'. When they said they were keen to push the boundaries, I thought 'Whoo hoo!', but I had to do some seriously hard thinking in order to deliver. Functionwise, the things that Jeff, Michele and their three girls wanted to do in the garden weren't too demanding. Entertaining, hanging out the washing, relaxing with a dash of gardening thrown in, were all that was being asked of this garden — all very easy to accommodate in such a generous space, but how to do it with topnotch panache?

Inspiration came when I saw whiz kid Australian garden designer Jack Merlo's 2004 winning entry for the Melbourne International Flower and Garden Show. With a stunning, wide-timbered deck that curved up into a complete perpendicular at one end, becoming a wall, the garden was a sculpture in its own right. This for me was the key: to give every element in the garden a sculptural presence; not just things like water features that lend themselves to being treated as a sculpture, but also less obvious things like steps and level changes.

With a direction in mind we could move forward. On a broad level the garden was going to remain divided into three zones, all flowing freely into one another. Naturally the Great Wall of Lattice was going to be removed, and with it gone, the space became huge and suddenly the garden was all about the two crepe myrtles.

A (fake) slate wall (right) conceals the garden shed and creates a beautiful textured backdrop. Shade is provided by the crepe myrtles and an aluminium and timber canopy. The fountain (far right) continues the play on the spiral shape. Its mosaic basin replicates the green tones in the *Buxus microphylla* surrounding it.

Zone 1 was the existing deck, which would remain more or less as is. Zone 2 was the back area which now had the potential to become a great lounging space taking advantage of the shade and beauty of the crepe myrtles. Zone 3 was the space between the deck and the laundry, a place to dry clothes, and principally a thoroughfare.

The boundaries were the first to be dealt with. Rather than tearing down the metal fences and ripping out the lollipop conifers, I thought it best to mask the fence and the ugly conifer trunks and at the same time take advantage of the privacy that the tops of the conifers were giving us. Eight of the conifers growing next to the crepe myrtles and clogging up their canopies were removed to allow the crepe myrtles a bit of breathing space. On the side where both the metal fence and conifers remained, the solution was to mask them by building a freestanding wall of treated pine clad with fibre cement cladding sheets. On the side where the conifers were removed, the fibre cement cladding sheets were attached directly to the metal fence. The metal shed, then, remained in its existing position and a freestanding masonry wall was built in front of it, masking the shed and at the same time providing a backdrop for the narrow end of the garden. The open-sided garage/laundry was simply boxed in, clad with more fibre cement sheets, with access maintained via a sliding door.

With the structure of the boundaries determined, it was time to fill in-between them. The means of getting down from the deck provided a good opportunity to develop the sculptural concept — and if I can avoid using a regular set of steps, I will. The idea was to have a series of generous platforms placed one atop the other, in a way that directed the flow and 'energy' of the space towards the end of the garden. It was important to pull out all stops to make sure the whole garden came to life, and the best way to do that was to encourage people to move through the entire space, not just parts of it.

Stepping off the existing deck, you move onto a new paved platform and then onto a long catwalk-like deck. This deck juts out,

SLATE

Stacked slate walls are very spunky additions to a garden, and work particularly well in a contemporary garden space. However, they are labour intensive and can be prohibitively expensive. Fake slate walls are a way of achieving the same look but at a much reduced cost. Slivers of stone are glued together to create a 'tile' of consistent size. The slate tiles (which are available in a wide range of colours) are then glued to a solid masonry wall. I repeat, a solid masonry wall! This is a material that falls into the 'too much of a good thing' category. Use it sparingly as a feature wall, otherwise it can be overwhelming.

GRAVEL

Gravels of all types create a nice visual texture and force you to experience the garden differently, slowing your pace and making that distinctive 'crunch' underfoot. Particularly when using light-coloured gravels, it's important to first lay geotextile fabric. This is a synthetic fabric which allows water to pass through it freely but will prevent the gravel from mixing and being dirtied by the soil it's sitting on. Keep the gravel no deeper than around 40 millimetres (1½ inches) otherwise you'll feel like you're wading through it rather than walking over it. When using gravel, be prepared to keep it clean by raking it free of leaves and other debris — many people find an electric blower useful for this task.

cantilevered over the lower paved platform on which it sits so that it 'floats', like a jetty above water. It is a place to sit and swing your feet under the shade of the crepe myrtle.

Moving off the lowest paved platform you enter the back section of the garden, and this was where we needed some bold but sublime elements. The first was a good old rendered-brick built-in seat, but this time I was upping the ante considerably and turning it into something with energized form — an undulating rhythmic 'snake' seat. At around 10 metres (33 feet) long it acts like a backbone to the space, 'stitching' the top and bottom areas together.

Above the snake seat is a simple but equally bold and sculptural element in the form of a shade canopy. Raked, falling to the rear of the garden, it plays with the perspective of the space and makes it appear larger than it is. With any pergola-esque structure it's important that it doesn't overwhelm the house, and the canopy's simple clean lines ensure it remains a slick piece of construction, while giving due respect to the house. (Using the same design and construction, a clothesline sits outside the laundry — a clothesline that only looks like a clothesline when there are actually clothes hanging on it.) Natural reed cladding is rolled up and down manually to provide shade as required.

Completing the triad of 'wow' components is the water feature. I hate this term water feature — it has to be one of the most token and frequently awful parts of thrown-together gardens these days. With this paranoia firmly ensconced in my head it was important that this w.f. be anything but token. To counterbalance the rectilinear elements throughout the space and as a partner to the curves of the snake seat, I figured that we needed something circular. The eventual idea was to create a very sculptural form with a shallow wok-like central basin, tipped slightly forward, encircled by shaped *Buxus microphylla*, transplanted from the front yard. The buxus were to be shaped so that the plants and the water basin were one continuous flowing form. The surface of the basin was then covered with mosaic, made up from a range of ceramic and glass green tiles chosen to match the range of green hues in the buxus. If you're going to have a water feature, naturally you've got to have some water — it was delivered via a proboscis-like copper water pipe which played on the spiral idea used throughout the garden.

The idea of reinterpreting the spirals used in the metal balustrades of the 1950s and 60s architecture was fully explored in the spiral screens. To simply copy some of the metal balustrades as they appear on the patios and front steps of the surrounding houses wouldn't get

Generous platforms (far left) are used in place of steps to try and make the level change more interesting and easier to traverse. The path to the garage and laundry is maintained (top left) but made less obvious by the patchwork of pavers, gravel and succulents (top right). The cantilevered deck (above) floats above the gravel.

The timber frame and steel spiral were inspired by the metal balustrades commonly found in the area.

the irony across — just like the breeze blocks in the inner city garden on pages 156–67. So by playing with the spiral shape, overenlarging it and abstracting the whole shape, I came up with the spiral screens. The spiral is a piece of flat bar which was bent to shape using a 1:1 template as a guide to get the shape just right. The spiral of flat bar was then cut into a hardwood timber frame — the shape of the timber frame itself being retro inspired, taking its cue from modernist painter Mondrian's square and rectangular compositions.

The smaller of the screens has a practical purpose: attached to the edge of the upper paved platform, it acts as a safety barrier. The larger screen is definitely the 'hero' screen, and positioned against the rust-coloured wall acts as one hell of a feature and focal point.

The third space in the garden outside the laundry and adjacent to the existing deck could have been another open area acting as an overflow zone. If I'd done that, however, it would have undermined the importance of the two other areas as gathering spaces. To ensure their success it was critical that this area be treated very differently. The best way seemed to be to use a grid, which would not introduce any new shapes to compete with the snake seat or the water feature but would simply reinforce the rectilinear thing that was going on. Grids are great tools: you can do different things in each part of the grid, but because of its overall logic and geometry, everything works and hangs together — just like a patchwork quilt. And that's exactly how this area was going to be treated — as a patchwork of 600 x 600 millimetre (about 2½ x 2½ inch) concrete pavers, succulents and pebbles. To bring the grid into the third dimension, buxus, which we rescued from the garden in its former state, was replanted occupying single, double or quadruple squares and trimmed to different heights. The area will always be a thoroughfare, with access maintained between the existing deck, laundry and clothesline, but the grid and all its components turn it into an arty garden carpet.

With so many things going on in this garden it was important that the palette of paint finishes, surface types and textures worked together. If not, we wouldn't have got past the issues the garden had in its former life. I wanted to keep this all pretty earthy but with some bold moments of colour. Rusted metal, stone and timber always make a killer combination. The only bummer is the cost and time you need for these materials to age and weather properly. Thankfully you can get around this by faking it. The masonry wall masking the metal shed was perfect for the new stacked slate tiles. These are genuine slate but come in pre-glued tiles that are then fixed to a masonry wall.

A perfect partner to the slate was going to be rust — rust paint to be exact. I've been a fan of this product for a while and was keen to try it out on a big scale. The freestanding wall behind the snake seat was perfect, but to break up the rust, the wall panels were separated

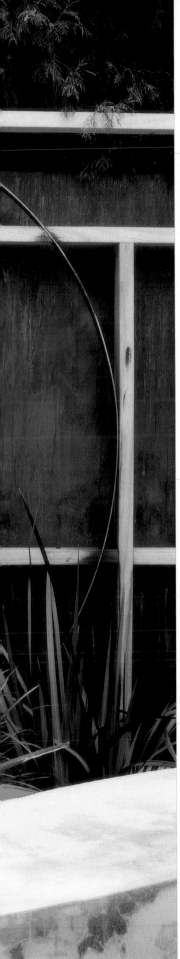

by narrow sections of natural reed cladding hung so that the reeds ran horizontally. The slate and rust became the dominant tones and textures in the space. Two bold colours then become a brilliant contrast — a lovely dirty red on the wall behind the crepe myrtles and a crimson pink next to the laundry behind the lemon tree.

Taking the floor of the garden into account palettewise is just as important, to ensure everything hangs together. Here I wanted to restrict it all to greys and whites with the exception of the natural timber on the catwalk deck. The dark grey and pale grey pavers create a very smart, but neutral, colour scheme that doesn't try to compete with any of the other colour or texture in the garden. The white quartz gravel (another favourite) creates a great not-too-hard, not-too-soft garden floor alternative that sets up a completely different mood to the other decked and paved spaces. The gravel slows your walking pace and so encourages you to take it easy. The even whiteness and reflectivity of the crushed quartz help to brighten shady areas as well as visually isolate each element — be it a plant, water feature or wall — allowing you to concentrate more on its shape, colour and texture.

To overplant this garden would be a mistake. With so many strong sculptural elements balancing each other in terms of an overall composition, it was important that the planting enhance this balance and not detract from or upset it. The crepe myrtles were undoubtedly the dominant natural/plant element in the garden. The planting needed a light touch — fine vertical lines and limited colour would be the direction. The name of the suburb, Kogarah Bay, comes from the Aboriginal term for 'place of reeds', and this offered some solid clues on what plants would be at home here and have some resonance and meaning. A walk around the area offered some choices that could work nicely: common rush, *Juncus effusus*, a grassy reed-like plant that is tough as old boots, as well as *Lomandra longifolia* 'Tanika' and *Dietes grandiflora*. These are plants you wouldn't give the time of day as you go past them in roadside plantings, but in the right surroundings their inherent design qualities can come to the fore. Himalayan weeping bamboo (*Drepanostachyum falcatum*) and the ginger *Alpinia caerulea* 'Redback' were included to add height to the planting scheme. I love the instant sanctuary-like quality that bamboo brings to a space — it has an elegance, calmness and serenity that is truly individual.

Concrete pots unearthed from auction houses and secondhand stores, and planted with succulents, reinforce the retro 1950s and 60s era look that the spirals refer to. The pots and succulents are a nice grounded contrast to the contemporary feel of the rest of the garden.

Although Jeff and Michele's garden has been reinvigorated with an undeniable contemporary flavour, the use of local elements as starting points for inspiration has ensured that it's a place that feels at home in the broader neighbourhood — and not like something that's dropped in from outer space.

RUST

Though the mere mention of rust strikes fear into the heart of car owners, the rich earthy tones of a rusty patina are nothing less than naturally occurring art! Rust paint available from specialist paint stores can be applied to virtually any surface and will fool everybody that the object in question is solid steel — albeit completely rusted. A couple of coats of the paint (which contains actual iron particles) is applied first and allowed to dry before a chemical rusting solution is applied over the top. A number of applications of this solution can be made until you have achieved the rust effect you desire.

A GARDEN OF STONE
AND WOOD

The stone buildings on the property (below left and centre far right) were built by the original Swiss–Italian settlers and faithfully restored by Carol White. Stone walls built around the property (right) offer a timeless connection at 'Lavandula' between the garden and the ground from which it was quite literally hewn.

A PLACE WITH SOUL

DESIGNED BY CAROL WHITE

FROM A PALETTE OF INSTANT RUST AND STONE, TO A
GARDEN BUILT AROUND THE REAL THING — WHERE
TIME AND PATIENCE GO HAND IN HAND

If there's one thing guaranteed to make me go weak at the knees, it's the combination of weathered timber and worn stone. Mix it with a bit of rusty steel and a few dozen lavender rows, and you have romantic imagery of the most irresistible kind.

Like me, Carol White is a bit of a soft touch for the stone and timber combo and bravely took on the mighty challenge of restoring the property 'Lavandula' (previously known as 'Shepdale') in the late 1980s. The collection of stone buildings and outbuildings were in a pretty sorry old state and it required a gritty determination to see the job through. Working only with the materials and construction techniques that the original Tinetti family would have used back in 1850s when they settled the area, Carol ensured that the heart and soul of this place remain intact.

The Tinetti family were part of a group of Swiss–Italians stranded in Victoria, unable to pay their return fare following a poor strike rate in the nearby goldfields. Determined to make the best of their circumstances they began growing grapes and producing sausages and cheeses like only they knew how. The houses they built were from the materials that surrounded them — timber and stone.

Stone and timber are the rawest and most elemental of building materials and together they are an unsurpassable combination. One complements the other, timber being warm in look and feel, and stone cool. Being of the earth, these materials always look connected to the place where they are being used — organic, uncontrived and unprocessed. By contrast, most plastics and some metals have a synthetic quality that will always be 'divorced' from the earth.

Though the original creators of this place did all they could to continue the culture and tradition of another place, the buildings they created and the legacy they left dovetail comfortably within what is a distinctively Australian rural landscape. They used stone from the local creeks and timber fallen from the surrounding trees, and so ensured that even

though the form and architecture of the buildings is clearly of European origin, there is the strongest sense that these buildings are of this place and of its earth.

In resuscitating 'Lavandula', Carol gave the place a whole new life as a lavender farm. Again, this use evoked European references, but it is still a component that sits comfortably in its Australian context. In full flight over summer, row upon row of lavender make a strong graphic statement, as endless purple stripes electrify the landscape. I've always been excited by the sight of lavender grown on a huge scale, resembling a large-scale artwork akin to the work of renowned American-based sculptor Christo, famous for wrapping entire coastlines or complete buildings in fabric.

Through each season the lavender has much to offer, and during the winter, pruned and shaped for the forthcoming flowering, the rows are at their most sculptural.

If you've read the chapter on the making of my mum and dad's garden at 'Campton' (pages 80–91), you might have already picked up on my penchant for the lavender row. I believe it's a European garden reference that transfers to an Australian context without a hint of jarring. The colours of the lavender — their purples, silvers, grey-greens and blue-greys — work harmoniously with the muted colour palette of the Australian bush. As a form of agriculture, it's a bit of a boutique 'glamour' crop, but that only helps to set it apart and make it a little bit more special, possessing that dual quality of being a practical thing to grow as well as being jaw-droppingly beautiful.

'Lavandula' is a place I walk around like a supermarket, thinking 'I'll take one of those stone buildings, some of that cobbled walkway, and half an acre of lavender'. The one indefinable quality that makes some places and gardens more appealing than others is soul. It's created through a combination of two essential things — the materials a place is hewn from, and the evidence of the human toil in doing so. Any place like 'Lavandula', built from stone and wood, whether it was built yesterday or two centuries ago, will possess bucketloads of soul. It's a quality that transcends fashion and fads, and once a place has it, it has it forever.

Winter is a low-key affair at 'Lavandula' compared with the colour (namely purple) and movement of spring and summer. But winter allows the bones of the garden to be revealed and is a time to fully appreciate the earthy textures and graphic forms.

The palette of materials for this garden is inspired by its coastal location. The owners' number one desire was for outdoor places to sit.

MOAR GARDEN 6

A FRONT GARDEN TO BE USED AND LOVED, WHERE THE SIMPLE ACT OF SITTING IS THE ONLY DESIRE TO BE SATISFIED, A SPACE TO RECEIVE THE SAME SORT OF ATTENTION NORMALLY LAVISHED ON THE BACK YARD, RESPONDING STRONGLY TO ITS BEACHSIDE PROXIMITY

BEACHFRONT

Right this minute, all around the world, there are front yards going to waste, just sitting there, being walked through a few times a day — and that's all! Someone with a balcony measuring 3 x 1.5 metres (10 x 5 feet) would kill (though I hope it doesn't come to this) for a bit of outdoor space the size of the average small front yard — a space at least four times the size of his or her balcony.

Yes I know they look lovely and they're all about making an impression and creating an entry, but what about using them — really using them.

It's a cultural thing.

The bulk of us are fairly uptight about sitting out in the front yard, and we should take a cue or two from our more community-minded Greek and Italian neighbours who happily while away the long summer afternoons taking in the passing action from their front verandahs. To my mind, having people engaging like this brings a street to life.

Geoff and Lindy Milne were halfway to agreeing with me on this one. While their Anglo heritage predicated that they weren't quite ready to fully engage with the passing parade on a permanent basis, they were pretty keen to make full use of their front yard.

Located in an enviable position, their home was a low-key beach house, sandwiched on a coastal peninsula between lagoon and ocean.

Slow and steady progress had been made on the house, with renovation happening as time and budget allowed. As far as potential goes, the front yard had it all over the back yard: the northeasterly aspect, the perfectly formed mature gleditsia in just the right position, and the not too big, not too small proportions — around 5 x 9 metres (16 x 30 feet) — were great raw ingredients.

Added to this were the improvements made to the house that addressed the front yard — namely the new double front doors and the generous deck and steps that ran its entire length. The simple addition of the deck already made the front yard a more useable space. The first time I visited Geoff and Lindy, I didn't make it past the steps of the deck — I don't even think I went inside. Not that Geoff and Lindy are bad hosts — far from it — it was purely that the deck and steps invited you to immediately sit and linger rather than travel further into the house.

CUES, CLUES, IDEAS, ELEMENTS, INSPIRATION
CHASING THE SUN COOL COLOURS SAND UNDERFOOT SURF
WELCOME ACCENTUATE THE HORIZONTALS PLEASE STAY
LOUNGE ABOUT TAKE A SEAT STRETCH OUT

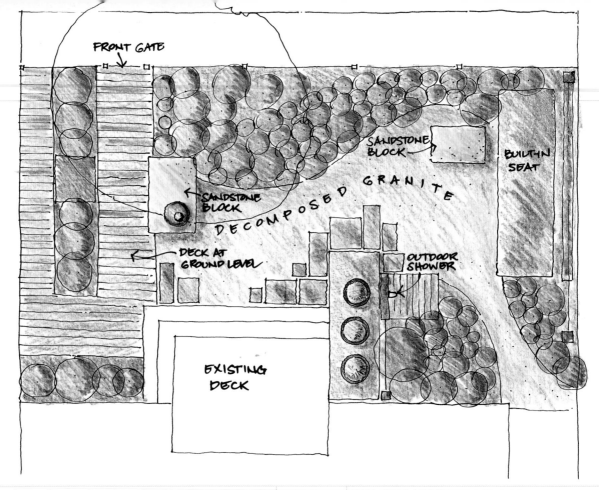

It was a completely satisfying, safe and comfortable space to be in. This was going to be easy.

The owners' only real requirements were that they be able to use their front yard — they just wanted it to be a place where they and their three children could spend a lot of time. In particular Lindy wanted to take advantage of the winter sun that the space received. The wish list also included a shower that the kids could use when they came back from the beach.

This was a nice, clear, simple, list of wants. Being clear about what you want to do in your space is the first vital step in garden creation. Principally it's all about determining the function of the space, and the key function to be conducted in this garden was sitting — being in the space, engaging and interacting with it. This sounds simple enough, but I find it surprising how often people wonder why they don't really use their garden when quite simply it's because there is nowhere to sit! If the options for sitting and lying down are totally irresistible, then your garden will be inhabited by people constantly — I guarantee it. It's precisely the same thing that happens when you see a big comfy couch or a sumptuously made-up bed — your laze-around instinct immediately kicks in.

Plantwise, Lindy was a big fan of grasses similar to those growing in a garden across the road. Feelwise, both Geoff and Lindy were very open-minded but keen for the space to suit both the house and the area. Both requests were music to my ears.

Tapping into a sense of place can sometimes be a very tricky thing indeed. Trying to identify what is special or unique about a place can

KEY PLANTS

TREES/SHADE
Gleditsia triacanthos
   (Honey locust)

SHRUBS/FILLER
Melaleuca incana

GRASSES/GROUNDCOVER
Festuca glauca (Blue fescue)
Lomandra longifolia 'Tanika'
Miscanthus sinensis
   'Gracillimus'
Pennisetum alopecuroides
   'Black Lea'
Poa poiformis 'Courtney'
Poa poiformis 'Kingsdale'

STRAPPY-LEAFED
Arthropodium cirratum
   (Rengarenga lily)
Astelia chathamica (Silver spear)

CLIMBERS
Hardenbergia violacea
   (Native sarsaparilla)
Pandorea jasminoides
   'Lady Di'

GRASSES

While grasses are great for filling up space in planting beds, they possess many other qualities that make them worthwhile inclusions in planting schemes. They're generally very drought tolerant and will survive in a wide range of soil conditions. They have a unique softness, visually and texturally unmatched by any other type of plants. Though generally soft in appearance they also possess a sense of vertical form, though not as severe as many 'architectural' spiky plants such as yuccas or phormiums. Grasses are great for creating mood in a garden, bringing a sense of movement as they catch the slightest breeze and also taking on a wonderful glowing appearance when backlit by the sun.

Rendered brick plinths and sandstone blocks (far right) create the seats, direct movement around the space and define its edges. Block-like shapes are repeated through the garden, giving real strength and presence to the space. The boardwalk (top right) links the front gate and driveway to the deck. Miscanthus sinensis (top left) creates a soft barrier between garden and driveway.

be a challenge when it doesn't appear to have many redeeming features or seems bland and uninspiring. With coastal environments, however, there is much to draw on. The strong relationship with the water and the associated natural environments provide ample points of inspiration — sand, water, waves, bleached colours, driftwood, grasses, dunes, horizons, the sense of space, the light and much more. These are all evocative elements that provide an almost infinite supply of design possibilities.

Beyond the desire to sit and enjoy the space there were a couple of other important factors to take into account. The owners' car was permanently parked in the front driveway and there was no intention of finding it a new home, so it was necessary to think of a way to accommodate a car in the garden without it being too overbearing. The other consideration was that of access and entry — creating a clear sense of entry to the house and garden as well as maintaining good access to the car.

In starting to play around with the design of this garden I knew I wanted to keep it simple and bold — using confident, uncomplicated elements generous in scale and free of fuss and superfluous detail — and at the same time understated. These qualities are at the heart of the beach landscape: a few simple components, sky, sand, water — bold, vast in scale, but at the same time possessing a subtle, understated colour palette.

With this firmly in mind, the desire for seating became the main driver of the design; and, in turn, built-in seating seemed the natural element to design around. Built-in seating has great potential for

Outdoor showers are well suited to gardens — taking a shower outside is fun. The water from this shower (right) is collected and drained into the garden to help irrigate it. The colour palette of both plants and hard materials is subdued (far right).

shaping a space. It can be a bold and graphic element that makes no excuses for being there — but when executed with simplicity and free of embellishment, it can be quite low key. My favourite embellishment-free version of built-in seating is the rendered-brick variety — these lovely pale grey blocks can suit almost any type of garden or house, being so neutral in shape, form and colour.

Up until this point I'd only ever used fairly conservatively sized built-in seating, but for this garden I though it was worth overscaling things. Placing a series of seats or blocks around the garden gave it strong structure and purpose as well as directing movement around and through the garden. The largest seat would go along the southern boundary and take advantage of Lindy's winter sun. At around 1 x 4 metres (3 x 13 feet) it would be like a huge stone (or ceremonial plinth), big enough for the whole family to bask on. Placing this seat at what was essentially the end of the garden was a surefire way of bringing the most neglected part of the space to life. A second built-in seat of similar proportions would be placed adjacent to the deck installed by the owners, finishing off the look of the deck by providing a much-needed 'shoulder', or edge, that would add a bit more bulk to the structure.

Two more 'blocks' were needed to visually pin down the corners of the space and provide extra seating as well as direct traffic through the garden. But rather than use more rendered brick versions it was time to introduce a contrasting finish or material. Huge blocks of squared-up sandstone were what was in my head and after a hunt around a few demolition yards I found a large stockpile of sandstone — old building foundations including some enormous blocks measuring around 1 metre x 80 centimetres (3 x 2¾ feet) wide, and 60 centimetres (2 feet) high. After a bit of sweet talking we managed to buy two of them and arranged for them to be delivered to the site. Getting them into position, however, was a whole other story involving a very maxed-out bobcat and a lot of crossed fingers.

FREESTANDING SCREENS

One of the most perplexing garden design problems is how to divide up the space. You want to avoid the blandness of a completely open space but you don't want to break up the garden so that it becomes cluttered and overcompartmentalized, cutting one area off from another. A good way to approach it is to follow the modernist's mantra 'form follows function'. When there is a reason for and an architectural logic in creating a division in the form of, say, a freestanding screen, it will never look odd, intrusive or out of place. Do you need to hide the bins? Do you need to create a safety barrier? And can your screen have a dual function?

The combination of timber decking, decomposed granite, sandstone and grasses is a direct response to this garden's beachside location.

When using concrete or rendered surfaces it's very important to use other materials to warm things up. Sandstone (or any type of stone) does this beautifully, and so does timber.

The timber deck was a great starting point and set up a nice precedent for more timber to be used through the garden. I've always liked the imagery of boardwalks as well as those timber and chain pathways that are laid along sand dune tracks. To connect the front gate to the deck and ultimately the front door, a new timber deck was constructed at ground level that ran flush up against the side of the driveway. You don't often see timber decks at ground level, mainly because they take quite a bit more work (decks at ground level require a cavity beneath them to allow for drainage and air circulation), but the effect is definitely worth it. There is something very special and different about ground level decks as opposed to regular decks that are set off the ground.

In order to further divide up the space and bring some vertical dimension to the garden, a couple of different screens were used. To reduce the impact of the ever-present car, a slot was left in the ground-level deck for a 'hedge' of tall grass. *Miscanthus sinensis*, a beautiful clumping grass that reaches around 1 metre (3 feet), with plume-like seedheads that are held aloft of the main clump, created a soft buffer to the car as well as forming a boundary to the northern edge of the space.

A timber screen using horizontal battens was devised to provide a vertical edge for the rendered brick 'shoulder' next to the existing deck. On its reverse was the shower for the desalination of beachgoers. The screen was then repeated behind the large built-in seat, in front of the existing paling fence boundary. This screen basically acts as the backdrop to the entire space, and had it just been left as the rundown paling fence the cohesion and overall aesthetic of the whole space would have been undermined.

Timber screens or fences with horizontal battens seem 'right' for coastal gardens and architecture. I have a theory that because the coast is so dominated by the horizon, horizontal lines — long lazy lines stretching out forever — are more at home here than verticals. The repetition of horizontal lines in small spaces also helps to improve the illusion of space.

This garden proved to be a good example of how the way in which you treat the 'floor' dictates the mood and feel of the space. Decomposed granite, which happens to be a favourite garden floor solution of mine, was perfect for this garden. Combined with the grassy planting scheme and the rendered and sandstone surfaces, it creates a very evocative seaside palette. Had we used turf or paving it would have been a very different garden. I find that decomposed granite is a nice halfway point between these materials — not too hard, not too soft.

Lindy already had a good sense of what she wanted to plant in the garden. Grasses and strappy-leafed things was the direction she wanted to take, and a walk around the neighbourhood, along the beach and down by the lagoon certainly reinforced this. The spinifex

covering the sand dunes and the reeds growing on the edge of the lagoon were among the most evocative coastal imagery. All we needed to do was capture a similar sense of simplicity and elegance and we'd have a planting scheme that totally nailed our sense of place.

The existing gleditsia provided plenty of shade, so I could simply concentrate on the ground-level planting. A mix of poas (native tussock grass) — *Poa poiformis* 'Kingsdale' and *Poa poiformis* 'Courtney' — creates the bulk of the planting. 'Kingsdale' has a lovely bluish tinge to it, while 'Courtney' is a more regular green. Planted together in a matrix/chequerboard pattern the two grasses create a subtle colour contrast. Poas are very low-maintenance grasses that can reach up to 60 centimetres (2 feet) in height and width and should be cut back hard when they start to look a bit scraggy — once or twice a year should do it. To add a nice vertical element plantwise, the miscanthus that have been used along the edge of the driveway are repeated through the rest of the garden. Because of its lovely upright habit this grass works well in the corners of spaces and at the back of planting beds. Among the many great things about miscanthus are the stages it goes through in its growing season. Producing fresh new growth in spring and early summer, and seedheads in late summer, the grass in its dried-off state over winter is particularly beautiful. The entire plant, with seedheads intact, dries to a straw colour, and looks amazing — this form will be maintained through winter until the new shoots appear at the base of the clump in later winter/early spring. At this stage you should cut the whole plant back to just above the new shoots.

Phormium 'Merlot' and *Astelia chathamica* with their wide, blade-shaped leaves add a little more structure and contrast to the whole scheme and ensure the mass of grasses doesn't take it too far in the soft and fluffy direction.

The simplicity of the planting scheme reflects the simplicity inherent in the vegetation that is characteristic of the nearby sand dunes and the edges of the lagoon. If you take a walk around the dunes and lagoon and then return to Geoff and Lindy's front yard, you get a clear sense that the garden is very much inspired by its immediate locale.

DECKING AT GROUND LEVEL

Decking at ground level can work to great effect. It's not seen as commonly as decking set up off the ground, and the main reason is the extra work required. Timber decking, whether made from timber or treated pine, cannot be laid directly onto the ground, where it would promptly rot and in the case of hardwood make a fine feast for termites. An air space of at least 300 millimetres (about a foot) needs to be maintained below the underside of the lowest joist or bearer by excavating below ground level and incorporating appropriate drainage (check with your council or local authority to see if they have any requirements regarding this air space). This is easier to achieve in free-draining sandy soils, as opposed to clay soils. Seek advice from a builder or decking contractor if you choose to do this yourself.

The challenge for Hugh in this garden was to make it as enticing as the view (below left). The planting scheme is a mix of exotic and native drought-hardy plants. Clipable plants such as westringia, helichrysum and teucrium are pruned and coaxed into organic, amoebic forms that wrap and wind their way around the tree trunks and the sculptural plants such as *Agave attenuata*, yuccas and cordylines (right and far right).

A DRY GARDEN

GOING WITH THE FLOW
DESIGNED BY HUGH MAIN

FROM A BEACHFRONT GARDEN CAPTURING THE ESSENCE OF COASTAL, TO A RIVERSIDE LOCATION WHERE THE PLANTING SCHEME PROVES THAT A DROUGHTPROOF GARDEN IS ANYTHING BUT DULL

As we hurtle headlong into the modern world, the effect we have on the environment becomes an unavoidable issue. With populations swelling, space is disappearing, and so too are many of our natural resources. Practising restraint and conservation on both a global scale and a local level are more important than ever: preservation needs to become habit. For many places in the world, the most fundamental of resources — water — is the number one concern.

The issue of drought is one that will never ever go away in Australia. In theory we know this is the driest continent on earth, but for some reason we'd really rather not accept it as a fact. One of humankind's most notable abilities is our capacity for denial: sometimes it works in our favour as a survival mechanism, and at other times it's our greatest downfall. In the case of drought, denial just leaves you thirsty. Gardens and gardeners get a lot of flack for being big water guzzlers. On the whole most gardeners (in Australia) are acutely aware of water conservation, but even so the temptation to splash water around when things get a bit dry is too hard to resist.

All this is definitely changing. There are big moves afoot to promote and encourage the planting of drought-tolerant plants. This doesn't mean, as many would assume, purely native plants; it also includes a wide range of plants that come from dry climates such as the Mediterranean and southern Africa, creating the potential for some pretty terrific planting schemes and combinations. Once we let go of the idea that it's all got to be verdant, green and flowery we'll start to see some dynamic, energized and original planting schemes that are much more in touch with an Australian aesthetic than ever before.

For Hugh Main, this dry issue was one of the overriding considerations for the rejuvenation of a waterside garden overlooking the Port Hacking River in New South Wales. Rather than seeing this as a constraint, Hugh took it as an opportunity to prove that drought tolerant doesn't mean dagsville.

Initially the biggest handicap this garden faced in starting its new life was the view, not from the garden but from the house: it was a stunner. From the main upper deck this house looked out over a mesmerizing view of river and national park — so mesmerizing that you'd momentarily lose all motivation to make the trek down the slope through the garden and finally to the water's edge. However, getting as close as

possible to water (and preferably in it) is an urge always too strong to resist, so inevitably the downhill journey would be made. Very simply, Hugh's challenge was to make the journey as beautiful as the destination.

This garden is a great example of going with the flow. It was a matter of working with the site and the things affecting and influencing it (including low rainfall) rather than against them. The rough goat track that led down to the water's edge was simply refined with a new concrete path and the crumbling sandstone retaining walls were repaired and reinstated.

Ultimately, though, it is the planting scheme that makes the garden a success, ensuring that it sits comfortably and harmoniously within its distinctly Australian surrounds.

As a starting point, Hugh had a mature canopy of native trees including banksias, angophoras and eucalypts to work with. Adding to this was a matter of selecting a palette of plants with foliage colour and texture that matched and blended with the signature tones of the existing native trees and neighbouring national park. Among the plants that Hugh chose to work in with the silvers, grey-greens and olives were teucrium, westringia, helichrysum, raphiolepsis and artemisia — his choice also influenced by the drought tolerance of each and every one of these plants.

It's one thing to select a list of plants that satisfy these requirements, but it's another altogether to put them together in an aesthetically sumptuous plant combo experience. The thing that sets Hugh's efforts apart from what could have been a stock standard 'drought-proofed' garden is the way he's turned the entire planting scheme into one big sculptural feast. The plants have been controlled and manipulated to strike a perfect balance between strong form and points of focus.

The attentive pruning and ongoing shaping of the shrubs, particularly the small grey-leafed helichrysum and the westringia, is the most captivating part of the whole scheme. These sculpted shrubs take on the most sensuous amoebic forms as they wrap and wind their way around tree trunks, sandstone boulders and each other. Punctuating these organic shapes are the pointy, strappy leaves of architectural plants including good old *Agave attenuata*, doryanthes and yucca.

In the early spring the garden is given a colour injection with the spectacular blue flowers of *Echium fastuosum*. It's quite a sight, but as the attention-grabbing blooms fade, the skilful play of muted colour, form and texture ensures this garden is an inspiring place to be any time of the year, perfectly at peace with everything that surrounds it.

The water's edge is too good to resist, so visitors have to be coaxed off the upper deck of the house and away from the view (left): the garden is now as beautiful as the destination. Hedging plants like helichrysum (left) and westringia are predominantly silver and grey in colour, blending well with the eucalypts, sandstone outcrops and the concrete used for the steps (left and top right). The spiky form of *Yucca filamentosa* (centre right) is used as a contrast to the organic shapes of the pruned shrubs.

MOAR GARDEN 7

A GARDEN DETERMINED TO OVERCOME THE CHALLENGES OF UGLY INTERNAL VIEWS AND COMPACT PROPORTIONS, PLAYING WITH OPTICAL ILLUSIONS, PAYING HOMAGE TO THE INNER CITY INDUSTRIAL SURROUNDS AND GETTING TO THE ESSENCE OF 'TROPICAL'

INDUSTRIAL STRENGTH

Our cities are undergoing huge changes. As the suburbs start to reach the outer limits of the land available for development, focus has turned inwards and it's the inner city areas, previously low on the list of desirable places to live, that are being reinvigorated with fresh energy.

Megan and Ant are a pair of inner city groovers typical of the new blood putting a spring into the step of these weary worn-down old suburbs. Suburbs where industry once had, or still has, a significant physical presence.

They bought their tiny worker's cottage, pokey and dark, in inner city Sydney a couple of years ago, then set about renovating it. Renovating these days means a pretty serious reworking of the rear area where house and garden meet — and if you can afford it, it's money well spent.

The outward push is a reflection of a general desire to capitalize on a climate geared towards outside living. This reworking can mean all sorts of options from a humble (well-placed) window looking out over the garden or the whiz-bang concertina floor-to-ceiling glass doors that slide away to nothing, removing all barriers between in and out. Megan and Ant went the whole hog, took the plunge and opted for the latter.

Twelve months of toil, a renovation baptism of fire, and the owners had themselves a pretty slick contemporary pad — perfectly set up for taking advantage of all an outdoorsy climate has to offer. The only problem was their little bit of the outdoors wasn't altogether tempting. The couple of metres (a bit over 6 feet) of (newly laid) blonde sandstone paving running along the back of the newly opened-up house was as far as they ever ventured. Beyond lay an unloved smattering of plants, a muddy lopsided lawn, a newly constructed carport and the standard (butt ugly) aluminium garden shed. It was a classic case of the back yard essentials, at their rawest and most aesthetically challenged, pitted against a super-smart house conversion. Something had to give!

Megan and Ant were certainly aware that their 'view' (namely their entire back yard) wasn't the best around town, but weren't sure what direction to take things. Megan had suggested tropical. But for me this suggestion is like a red rag to a bull.

CUES, CLUES, IDEAS, ELEMENTS, INSPIRATION
OPTICAL ILLUSION MANIPULATE PERSPECTIVE COOL GREEN
CONCRETE LOOK CLOSELY MORE CONCRETE
APPRECIATE THE OVERLOOKED EDGY RIGHT UNDER YOUR NOSE

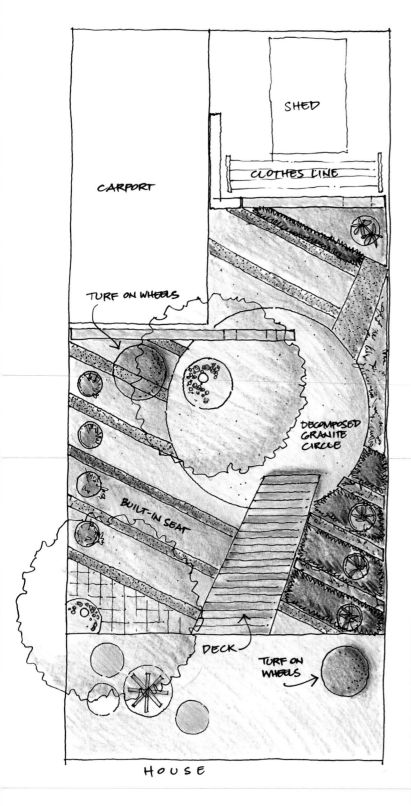

Whenever someone starts talking in strong style labels, I want to get to the heart of what they really mean. If you start talking final looks straight up, you can miss a lot of opportunities along the way. You've got to crawl before you can walk.

I was pretty sure Megan didn't mean she wanted a bit of Bali transplanted verbatim into inner Sydney. For me, and I've said this a few times now, this sort of approach takes you into Disneyland territory. Balinese gardens are fantastic — in Bali. I certainly don't see a problem with taking the essence of something from somewhere else with a distinctive style, as long as it is reinterpreted and given a very localized twist. It's getting back to that sense of place thing — trying to make gardens feel like they belong to where they are.

My hunch was right. Megan wasn't after a thatched roof gazebo overrun by an army of Buddha statuettes. Instead, she was after the essence of tropical — a feeling. She wanted a place that was sanctuary-like, cool and green, shady and leafy. When you think about it, that's a pretty standard desire. Free of the shackles of a locked-in style stereotype, we could move forward with the potential to take the garden in all sorts of directions.

So what were the best things about the garden in its current state? The best bit really was the inside–outside connection already set up by the owners. As for the garden, well, it was reasonably level and it had good potential proportions: around 7 x 7 metres (23 x 23 feet) — a good room-sized space.

On the down side we had that carport and garden shed just sitting there, looking ugly, not planning to go anywhere. There was no plant life of any value and the paling fences running down either side of the space were mismatched and not running level or square to the house. Not that I'm suggesting that paling fences need to be perfect and square and level, but in such a small space — and particularly with such a slick house renovation — the lack of level and squareness can be very disconcerting.

On the broadest level it was clear we needed to improve the view by blocking out the current one. Some type of wall or screen was needed to conceal the carport and the garden shed. Beyond that it was a matter of fulfilling the desire for cool and green. This is always the point where I take a big gulp and hope for some divine inspiration.

CONTAINING THE BEAST

Black bamboo (*Phyllostachys nigra*) is one of the loveliest bamboos, but being an invasive variety (there are two varieties of bamboo: clumping and invasive or running) it needs to be contained. For one half of this garden, narrow 600 millimetre (about 2 feet) deep galvanized planters were custom built and lined with a polyethylene root barrier to contain the bamboo. Along the other edge a stormwater pipe was cut into sections to create planters. Cutting the pipe up is not a job for the faint hearted — a demolition or concrete saw is required and should only be handled by an experienced operator.

Black bamboo in galvanized planters (top right) screens the fence. Masonry walls conceal a carport and shed, while false vanishing points created by a deck with converging parallels (bottom right) make the space seem bigger. The turf on wheels (below) was created with tongue firmly in cheek.

KEY PLANTS

TREE/SHADE/FEATURE
Plumeria sp.
  (Pink frangipani)

SCREENING
Phyllostachys nigra
  (Black bamboo)

FILLER/GROUNDCOVER
Liriope muscari 'Evergreen
  Giant'

FOLIAGE/FLOWERING
Canna 'Tropicana'

FOCAL POINT
Agave attenuata
  (Century plant)

That never works, so the next best thing is to take a walk around the block.

It's my mantra — the clues to making your space unique and special are invariably surrounding you, right under your nose. Walking around Megan and Ant's turf is all about concrete and steel — worn-out concrete and rusty steel. For me, always a great starting point. These are things that you'll walk past every day and most likely treat with disdain, but if you look, and I mean really look, you'll find these things possess lovely textures and qualities in their own right. The exposed aggregates of age-weary concrete, the impressive scale and proportions of steel columns and girders typical of old industrial areas, are among the elements that can inspire a palette to draw upon for inner-city garden creation.

One element that I couldn't ignore was the old concrete breezeblocks. Remember them? They were all the rage in the 1950s and 60s and they're everywhere around the inner city, used as front fences, screens and even entire walls. They were conceived as part of the concrete block system that was a post-war alternative to the clay brick. The idea behind the breezeblocks, as their name suggests, was to allow ventilation through otherwise solid walls. They're another element common in the inner city that you could be forgiven for dismissing as pretty damn ugly. But again if you put on those fresh eyeglasses you can see they have a great graphic quality to them. I was sure they could have a place in the garden, but when transplanting items that are as iconic (and as common) as these, it's important to reinterpret them and give them a real twist in order to get the irony and bring out their latent design qualities. The question was, how?

One other pertinent question was what the owners wanted to do in the garden. They're a pretty chilled-out couple, and chilling out was exactly what they wanted to do in their garden. Simple!

With all the factors now in the melting pot, it was a matter of working up a design. The broad concept was this: to improve the boundaries all round by building a couple of solid walls to conceal the sheds and improving one of the paling fences by cladding it to look

DECOMPOSED GRANITE
Decomposed granite is a material that creates a surface similar to that of a country dirt road. Like gravel, it's a nice intermediate garden floor surface that is firm without being as hard as paving. In order to stabilize the surface of the granite you can ask your supplier to mix some dry cement into the load, which helps the top layer to 'set'. Be conscious when you locate decomposed granite that it's not hard up against the house, otherwise you will forever be leaving dusty footprints inside your home.

Through winter, when the frangipani has shed its leaves, its sculptural trunk is shown off to full effect in front of the sky blue wall. The decorative breezeblocks (far right) are an element that characterize the local area. Here they are presented with a sense of irony, turned into a focal point with coloured translucent Perspex sandwiched between them to create a retro stained glass wall.

like a masonry wall; to provide some built-in seating; and to include as much plant material as we could — all while trying to make the space seem as big as possible.

My first thoughts were to make it a pretty simple space of right angles heading in a minimalist direction, responding to the house. This approach could have been okay, but it seemed a bit stock standard and wasn't responding to the individuality that Megan and Ant both exude. Using the desire to make the garden space look as big as possible became the trigger for taking this design into an interesting area.

Optical illusions — tricks that you're more likely to see used in theatre design — became the order of the day. Two simple concepts were employed in the construction of the masonry walls used to conceal the carport and garden shed. Firstly, they were staggered (to allow access to the carport) and secondly, the rear wall was made slightly shorter in height than the front wall. The staggering of the walls and their differing heights cheat the perspective and suggest a greater depth to the garden, as well as fooling visitors into thinking the garden continues around behind the wall. Though you quickly discover you're simply delivered into the carport, the psychological suggestion that the space is larger remains.

Canna 'Tropicana' (above) is planted in cut-down stormwater pipes to give a colour injection beyond the painted walls. The oranges and reds of the foliage are a great contrast against the purple and blue of the walls. The black bamboo (top right and far right) is mulched with small-grade blue metal.

The overall layout, rather than being square to the house, was skewed by about 30 degrees, and a false vanishing point was created by converging the parallel lines of a timber deck, which point towards the staggered purple rear wall.

Viewing the design from overhead, stripes of contrasting width reinforce the skewed layout. At ground level the stripes take the form of dark grey painted concrete alternating with narrower pale grey concrete strips featuring an exposed aggregate — picking up on the concrete surfaces in the surrounding streets and roads. The stripes then become three-dimensional, in the form of a large built-in rendered concrete seat and custom-built galvanized planters containing black bamboo (*Phyllostachys nigra*).

The timber deck steps down onto a circle of decomposed granite that is home to one of the garden's (future) features — a pink-flowering frangipani (*Plumeria* species). The layout of the circle is another visual trick to make the garden seem larger. It wraps around behind the purple wall, suggesting that the garden continues around also. Had the circle appeared in its entirety in front of the wall the effect would not have been achieved. The combination of the deck and decomposed granite circle also serves to soften and add warmth to the space, contrasting against the concrete and metal planters.

SIMPLE PLANTING SCHEME

If you're overwhelmed by the idea of planting out a garden, err on the side of simplicity. You often only need three or four kinds of plants. Provided they are all doing different jobs, you can attain enough contrast between them to keep things interesting. In this garden there are five plants in total: (1) frangipani (*Plumeria* species) for tree cover and shade, (2) black bamboo (*Phyllostachys nigra*) for screening and setting the mood of the garden, (3) *Liriope muscari* 'Evergreen Giant' as a groundcover and space filler, (4) orange-flowering *Canna* 'Tropicana' with multicoloured striped foliage for a dash of foliage and flower colour, and (5) *Agave attenuata* as a focal point.

The step down from the deck is an additional (subtle) method of making the space appear larger. It's only one step, but it adds a greater dimension to the space than an entirely level surface would have done. Similarly, if the split level had stepped upwards at the back it would appear to be bearing down on you rather than opening out.

The breezeblocks found their place in the garden — in fact, they became the focus of the entire space. There were potentially two ways of using them to ensure that the irony of having them in the garden came through loud and clear. Either they could be used en masse to create overwhelming walls of breezeblock, or a small number only could be featured to deliberately draw attention to the blocks. I opted for the latter. Breezeblocks were inserted in both backdrop walls, with alternating coloured Perspex sandwiched between a double layer of blocks, and became focal points that made a clever reference to the surrounding neighbourhood. During the morning and the middle of the day, the colour of the Perspex is not so apparent, but as the afternoon wears on, the low angled light makes the Perspex glow brilliantly, creating a pair of retro stained glass windows that completely steal the show.

The one thing you have to try to talk people out of more than anything else is a lawn. Ant was pretty keen on maintaining some link to one of the greatest of our suburban icons. Thankfully he didn't need a great deal of convincing that it was time to let go of this grassy fantasy. His three attempts at turfing have all ended with the same muddy result. A friend had told me of a mobile lawn she had seen in a book on contemporary landscapes. Despite much harassment (by me) she was unable to find the book, but the idea of a mobile lawn was enough. All of the corrugated iron around the area made it clear that cut-down water tanks on wheels were an almost obvious solution. When we first filled them with soil and laid the turf over them, we couldn't believe how perfect they were: irreverent, quirky, spunky, completely original while giving that lovely softness that only a lawn — or a bit of one — can bring to a space. If they appeal to you, just be aware that they take precisely the same amount of maintenance that a regular lawn needs — just on a smaller scale.

And what of Megan's tropical desires? This garden is a great example of how you can still achieve the feeling or essence that you want without being a slave to the look or style that normally delivers it. The form and layout of this garden is a direct response to the needs of the owners while making strong connections with its surrounds. Using generous amounts of black bamboo, with a few canna lilies and a carpet of liriope, the space is surrounded and engulfed by greenery and colourful foliage. The two frangipanis will in time create some welcome shade while the flowers — particularly the ones against the azure blue wall — will satisfy any tropical yearnings.

Megan and Ant's garden is proof that even in what would initially appear to be the most un-garden-friendly of places, there is inspiration to be sought that can create exciting original spaces. Spaces that acknowledge where they are, and which also provide a sanctuary to escape to.

The circular shapes of the stormwater pipes and turf on wheels (left) act as a foil for the rectangular concrete strips on the garden floor as well as for other angular elements including the rendered brick seat, the deck and the metal bamboo planters (above).

The crisp clean edges of the built-in furniture and contemporary designer pieces are softened by the glossy dark green foliage of *Trachelospermum jasminoides* and *Cycas revoluta* (right). Dwarf forms of *Magnolia grandiflora* 'Little Gem' line the boundary (top far right). A restrained palette of hard materials creates a slick contemporary space (centre far right). Deciduous (non-fruiting) pear trees shade the space (bottom far right).

A GARDEN FOR OUTDOOR LIVING

STREAMLINED

DESIGNED BY JACK MERLO

FROM AN OUTDOOR ROOM IN TOUCH WITH ITS INDUSTRIAL SURROUNDINGS, TO ANOTHER THAT IS A CLEAN, CRISP EXTENSION OF THE HOME IT PARTNERS

Welcome to the outdoor room. To some it's the epitome of contemporary outdoor living — to others it signals the very downfall of century-old gardening traditions. Who would ever think such divisive controversy swirled through the world of gardens?

You see, gardeners are very clever at lulling you into thinking they're lovely, amiable friends-of-the-earth types — but suggest replacing that veggie patch with a lap pool and all hell will break loose. Modern, minimal design is a great one for polarizing people's tastes — and it, like anything else, is subject to lively debate and criticism.

This whole outdoor room bizzo, however, didn't just pop up in the last couple of years. It started back in the 1920s and was fine-tuned in the 50s in California by a chap called Thomas Church. He was a champion of the key components of the outdoor room: establishing a seamless connection between in and out, providing paved areas close to the house for versatile dining and outdoor living spaces, and using a simple palette of plants that were chosen relative to the inhabitants' skill (or total lack thereof) in 'gardening'.

With the rise and rise of garden media — books, television shows, magazines and radio — 'the outdoor room' is now part of everyday garden speak. Pretty much everyone is up to speed on what outdoor rooms are, and there's a whole new generation of brown thumbs who've realized there's a way that they too can get the most out of their outdoor space without going into horticultural meltdown.

Jack Merlo is certainly no brown thumb; in fact he comes from good straight up and down gardening lineage. In a very short time, however, he's shot to prominence as one of the new breed of garden designers who are eager to explore all the design potential that the outdoor room concept has to offer. A big fan of the clean lines of contemporary architecture, Jack has carved quite a name for himself in designing gardens that are perfectly partnered with the slickest of modern architectural edifices.

Beyond the razor-sharp lines and right angles, the thing that is typical of Jack's designs is his carefully controlled palette. The colour, texture, shape and form of materials, hard or soft, are given the same careful consideration as the buildings that these spaces partner. Colour is rarely garish and is generally a pretty sophisticated combination of neutrals, the colour palette itself derived from, and matching, the range of building materials in their 'natural' finishes — the greys, browns and creams of stone, concrete and timber.

I'm always impressed when someone is able to exercise restraint in garden design (something I struggle with), and Jack has it down to a tee. The paring back of contemporary spaces dispenses with any frills and indulgent decoration, with function reigning supreme over all else. And the function of this Melbourne garden is clearly to be a place where you can dine, swim, be shaded on command and do it all with a minimum of fuss within a sparklingly crisp, clutter-free, space-efficient environment.

Perhaps the biggest gripe your gardener's gardener has with these whiz-bang modern places is that there is nowhere to 'garden'. But then again, that depends on what you define as gardening. If 'to garden' is to tend and nurture plants, then that is undoubtedly happening here. There are plants, and they definitely need nurturing, it's just that the plants don't look like they need to be helped along a great deal. The plants here are just as strong and forthright as any other component of this garden. Cycads, *Magnolia grandiflora* 'Little Gem', *Gardenia radicans*, Chinese star jasmine (*Trachelospermum jasminoides*), lillypillies (*Acmena smithii*) and strelitzias are all either strong in form or have solid green glossy foliage. The presence of the plants takes the edge off the sharpness of the retaining walls, paving and built-in furniture — but only just.

Is this the garden of the future? It definitely would be a hot contender. But it should also be regarded as one of the many gardens of the future. The best thing about the emergence of this approach to garden making is that it allows a whole new audience, mostly a younger one, to think about getting outside and finding their own way of interacting with the outdoor elements. When all is said and done, I'm certain that the venturing outside bit is the most important thing.

The fundamentals of shade and entertaining are designed into the space with built-in elements such as the custom-made furniture and the retractable shade awning (left). Verner Panton plastic chairs, design classics, add a contrast to the sharp rectilinear lines of the space. The garden is a good match for the contemporary house it partners (top right). The pool was retrofitted to suit the new garden (centre right). Lillypillies (bottom right) line the entrance, underplanted with *Cycas revoluta*.

Surrounded by eucalypt forest, this garden soaks up the view while many of its elements are inspired by the view and all that it contains.

A GARDEN OF BLURRED BOUNDARIES ENGULFED BY NATURAL BUSHLAND WHERE TREE TRUNKS, BARK AND SPIDER WEBS INSPIRE PLAYFUL CONTEMPORARY ELEMENTS — A PLACE ADVENTUROUS AND BOLD IN DESIGN BUT ALWAYS SYMPATHETIC TO ITS SURROUNDS

MOAR GARDEN 8

SPIRITED NATURE

Lou and Anthony are both artists who bought their home in the Blue Mountains outside Sydney about two years before I came onto the scene. Their house is one of five timber cottages with steeply pitched roofs, built side by side in staggered formation along a moderately steep slope overlooking a small valley. They were instantly taken with the charm and location of the group of houses, which could be mistaken for a mountain ski village.

While the houses were built to take advantage of the view and capitalize on the experience of being surrounded by natural bushland, the building process hadn't been completely sensitive to this concept. The area that counted as Lou and Anthony's garden was no more than a muddy scar — a muddy scar right next to some lovely bush — but a muddy scar nonetheless.

Without doubt this would have to be the most difficult garden I've ever designed. While it had a stunning outlook and the potential certainly seemed to be there, it was pretty hard to get past the muddy scar thing — oh and the two concrete septic tanks which were smack bang in the best part of the 'garden'. The outlook was interesting: it wasn't an expansive view out to the horizon, it was more two-dimensional. You looked out onto the opposite side of the valley which filled your field of vision — it was like bush wallpaper! Naturally, standing on top of the septic tanks was the best place to take in this bushy experience. Once again the crappiest thing in the garden got the best position.

The owners had cogitated on what their garden could be for the past couple of years and they'd come up with some pretty out-there ideas that made even me raise an eyebrow. In essence they were after a garden that was an artistic response to the bush that surrounded them.

An artistic response? I was all ears.

When you're creating a garden that's on the edge of a natural, relatively undisturbed reserve, there are a number of ways you can approach it. The first is to ignore it altogether and create something that is completely separate from all that surrounds it — paying it no heed in form, feel or plant choice. I'd hasten to add this is a pretty outdated attitude. Perhaps the most sensitive approach is to treat a garden such as this one like a bush regeneration project, using only

CUES, CLUES, IDEAS, ELEMENTS, INSPIRATION
SOAK UP THE VIEW FRAME IT EXPLORE THE POSSIBILITIES
TALL SMOOTH TRUNKS GREAT BALLS OF WIRE TANGLE OF BRANCHES
DANCING VERTICALS BARK WEAVING BUT IS IT ART

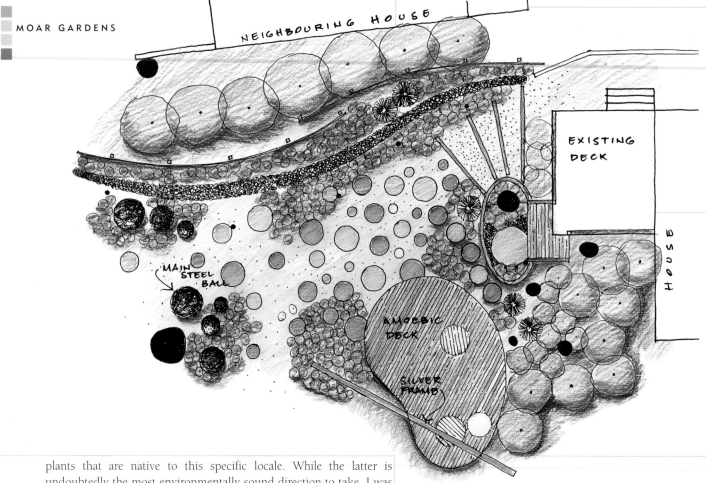

NEIGHBOURING HOUSE

EXISTING DECK

HOUSE

MAIN STEEL BALL

AMOEBIC DECK

SILVER FRAME

plants that are native to this specific locale. While the latter is undoubtedly the most environmentally sound direction to take, I was more excited by the artistic thing.

I need not have looked any further than the work of UK landscape sculptor/maestro/genius/god, Andy Goldsworthy. If you've never picked up a book on his work you are simply missing out. He creates ephemeral works in natural settings, using only what nature provides. Sticks, leaves, stones, earth, ice and water are his palette. His creations range from impressive spheres pieced together by shards of thawing ice, to mysterious circular holes in the ground created by a carpet of autumn leaves laid to form a perfect gradation of colour, from yellow through orange to red. These are stunning works that demonstrate the poetic skill of a man inspired by the poetry of nature. In other words, Andy's not pretending he hasn't been there: he's leaving his mark, albeit temporarily, in a way that is sensitively artistic and very beautiful.

I wanted this to be a garden that was a special spot for humans within the bush, to create bold original elements, inspired by and responding to the natural landscape that engulfed the site. I wanted to apply the basic premise of bush regeneration, using only species that occurred locally — but using them in a contemporary, fearless and confident setting.

Lou and Anthony were up for it and ready for the ride. This was going to be fun!

In addition to the septic tanks hogging the best spot in the garden, there were a couple of other issues to solve. That good old connection between in and out was only halfway to being good. From the main

KEY PLANTS

TREES/SCREENING
Elaeocarpus reticulatus
  (Blueberry ash)

SHRUBS
Banksia marginata

FOCAL POINT
Xanthorrhoea australis
  (Grass tree)

GRASSES/GROUNDCOVER
Gahnia sieberiana
Poa labillardieri
  (Tussock grass)
Poa sieberiana

FLOWERING
Actinotus helianthi
  (Flannel flower)

MAKING WIRE AND STEEL BALLS

Constructing the wire and steel balls in the garden was relatively simple. For the smaller galvanized wire balls, hoops of wire of matching diameter were made and then wired together in the same fashion as the longitudinal lines of an armillary sphere. Using this as a base, smaller hoops of varying diameters were then attached to build up the random appearance. The large steel ball was constructed using the same idea but on a slightly larger scale. Steel reinforcement rod was bent into circular hoops and then welded together. The steel is untreated and has been left to rust up.

The large steel ball (top left) is made from steel reinforcement rod and provides a dramatic focal point at the end of the garden (top right). A grass tree, *Xanthorrhoea australis* (bottom right).

living space of the house you stepped out onto a medium-sized deck — that bit was good. The flow from deck to garden — that bit was bad. There were a couple of steps to one side of the deck, but your natural impulse was to go to the opposite corner that looked out to our view. In garden design you should always give in to that initial natural impulse. Added to that, the drop from this part of the deck to ground level was around 1.8 metres (6 feet) — that's a lot of steps, so I needed to find a way of encouraging people to get off the deck and not be hindered by such a big level change.

The other matter to come to terms with was the boundaries: there were none. There was of course the neighbouring house to the north-west of the space that formed a backdrop to the garden, which I definitely needed to take into consideration, but apart from that there were no perceivable boundaries. This is very rare these days, and in a setting like this on the edge of a natural reserve was something to play to full advantage, so as to completely blur the boundaries — making it difficult to tell where garden ends and the natural bushland begins.

With strengths and weaknesses identified, and a very solid direction in mind, we could begin designing a garden.

First step was back to those septic tanks — until I worked out how to deal with them, this garden wasn't going anywhere. The tanks were definitely the best spot to take in the garden and the outlook, so it seemed logical that we capitalize on this and make it the heart of the space. A platform of some type over the top of the tanks that still allowed all the necessary access to them seemed to be the logical solution to this situation.

The silver frame (right) was originally intended to be red. Once built, it instantly became clear that it should remain silver. The desired effect of framing the outlook was achieved and the silver colour was a link to the silvery trunks of the eucalypts. Although the septic tanks once had the best spot in the garden, the deck has now assumed that privilege.

As I played around with forms, an amoebic timber deck started to evolve, with a kidney shape the eventual choice. For me, this shape then set a tone for the rest of the garden: freeform kidney shapes are reminiscent of the 1960s — a period of design that was playful and irreverent, an attitude I wanted to carry through the whole garden.

Now the idea of a deck over a couple of septic tanks is a straightforward enough concept, but the reality is something quite different. Local council had some pretty stiff requirements that we had to abide by. Support posts could be no closer to the tanks than 1 metre (3 feet) and they needed to penetrate the ground as deeply as the tanks themselves: this meant holes about 1.8 metres (6 feet) deep. We needed to allow clearance of 100 millimetres (4 inches) between the bottom of the bearers and the tank, plus everything had to be constructed from flame-retardant hardwood. To comply, the deck became bigger, higher and naturally more expensive.

Beyond solving the septic tank issue, the next biggest design challenge was how to link the existing deck attached to the house and the new kidney-shaped deck. In the end the difference in level between new and old deck was about 1.4 metres (4½ feet), and that would have meant eight or nine steps. I'm a believer that that's too many for your regular garden punter, so once again I chose to break the levels into bite-sized chunks: four steps, a platform for a break, then another three or four steps, and then you'd be down enjoying the new deck. This is all completely psychological, but it can be the difference between a garden full of people or a garden that is given the quick once-over from the back door.

The platform in this case was an elliptical-shaped brick planter that wrapped around the trunk of the existing ribbon gum (*Eucalyptus viminalis*). The ellipse was a perfect intermediate shape, moving from the rectangular deck to the kidney-shaped deck. To ensure minimal harm to the tree, large rocks, akin to railway ballast, were used to fill around the trunk, allowing a free flow of moisture and air to the roots below.

The steps from the platform down onto the deck were a nod to the circle idea that is played out through the garden, generated initially by the circular septic tanks. Steps and level change are a great chance to explore some sculptural alternatives — but what to use for perfectly formed freestanding circular steps? Stormwater pipes of course. Arranged like stepping posts in a playground, each of these pipes was topped with one of the circular pavers used through the garden.

With these issues solved, the rest of the garden was about blurring the boundaries and injecting big doses of artiness into the space.

The neighbouring house never really bothered me that much — it definitely had a strong presence in the space but I never felt like I

CREATING FRANKENSTEIN

The Frankenstein trees (as they became known) were simple to construct. Steel reinforcement rod was bent to shape in varying shallow curves, and small whimsical curls finished off the tops. The ribbon gum (*Eucalyptus viminalis*) saplings that were removed prior to the excavation work were sliced up into varying lengths and a hole drilled through their centres. These were then strung onto the curved steel rods one piece at a time and a galvanized steel hexagonal nut welded on the underside of each timber disc to support it.

wanted to screen it out altogether and pretend it wasn't there. It was more of a case of coming up with something that was unmistakably part of our garden, that paid respect to the neighbouring house, but also directed your attention back out to the view. This could have simply been a planting solution, but I saw this as an opportunity to start playing with the melding of art, the functional and the stylizing and reinterpretation of the surrounding bush.

Lou had thought she'd like to use the plentiful strips of bark that the ribbon gum shed periodically and weave them into screens — a nice idea but more on the ephemeral side of things that would've screamed Burn me! Using that idea as a starting point, I had in my head a curved timber screen made up from a collection of reclaimed and second timbers stacked atop each other, running horizontally, the different timbers echoing the long strips of bark. To add some light, colour and sex appeal to the whole screen I wanted to incorporate long, thin strips of coloured Perspex, aluminium and mirrored stainless steel. The timbers proved hard to source, and so we opted for new timber that matched the timber used in the kidney-shaped deck. Putting all this together was very much a case of doing a bit and then standing back to see how the whole composition was coming along. Using the new timber as opposed to reclaimed material turned out to be a blessing, as it was a perfect match for the bark on the trees as well as the timber colour of the neighbouring house.

Previously there had been ongoing erosion problems, with washouts across the site, so we needed some type of drain to carry the water away. One solution to this problem is to create a dry creek bed,

but I opted for something that was a little simpler and more graphic — basically a thick textured line that echoed the alignment of the curved bark-inspired screen. Very simply, a ditch was dug, a slotted drainage pipe line laid and railway ballast filled over the top.

The way in which the floor of this garden was treated was the key to blurring the boundaries. It was generally up to the planting, creating a carpet of the grasses and smaller flowering Australian natives that were growing naturally in the adjoining bushland — so continuing the forest floor planting right up into the garden. Identifying the plants that make up the forest floor can be tricky, and it's best to use either a native plant field guide or seek out the most knowledgeable person at your local nursery. While I wanted to have something of the richness and plant variety that was occurring just a stone's throw away, I was keen to be selective and choose the ones with the best design appeal. This was a mix of *Poa sieberiana*, *Poa labillardieri* and *Gahnia sieberiana*, and flannel flowers (*Actinotus helianthi*). The grasses are a piece of cake to grow and will cope with a wide range of conditions, but flannel flowers are definitely fussy though beguiling little creatures; the main issue is good drainage.

The planting was one half of the garden floor, the other half was the bit that you can walk on. This was always going to be decomposed granite and something. The something became circular concrete pavers. The pavers act like stepping stones through the granite, with the circles generated by and relating to the kidney-shaped deck. The circles sprinkled through the garden foster the fun and irreverence set up by the deck.

The way the garden floor was treated was instrumental in maintaining a link between the garden and the adjacent bushland. Decomposed granite and native grasses create a continuous carpet of earth and vegetation (left). Dissected saplings (above) are threaded along steel reinforcement rod to create the 'Frankenstein trees'. The screens (top right) form a backdrop to the space and were intended not to block out the neighbouring house but rather to divert attention away from it.

Bringing the circles into the third dimension are the spheres of wire and steel. Wire in all shapes and forms is a common element through Australian bushland, representing in some respects the control we try to exert over a natural landscape. The balls of wire were an attempt to stylize this iconic material, creating a sculptural element that could be repeated through the garden. The largest of the balls is made of steel reinforcement rod and creates a much-needed focus at the end of the space. The combination of the balls' lightness and their random tangle of steel and wire plays on the tangle of tea tree and banksias, as well as cobwebs and general bush debris that surrounds the garden.

One of the key things that Lou and Anthony responded to when they first saw this property were the trees. They're pretty hard to ignore — tall, white, perfectly straight trunks that dominate the landscape. Lou had wanted to find a way of representing them and had always liked the idea of totems in the garden. Before we began work on the garden there were some small skeleton-thin ribbon gum saplings that had to be removed. I thought we could cut them up as they normally would be when tree clearing, and reassemble them along a spine of steel reinforcement rod — effectively giving them a second chance at being part of this garden. Hence they were coined the Frankenstein trees. I think they're one of the most successful elements in the garden; they add a great sense of whimsy and bring something quite primitive yet elegant to the space.

On the very first visit to the garden, while standing on the septic tanks, Anthony had mentioned how he'd thought it would be great to frame the view with a red frame. I thought it was pure genius and was determined to make sure that was exactly what we did. In the end it stayed silver. I was ready to paint the aluminium frame red, but when push came to shove it made the statement and did the job without the extra help of colour.

To help the transition from the circular pavers to the spheres, I was after something to bridge the gap — almost as if the pavers were rising out of the ground and turning into spheres themselves. At first I considered somehow forming-up concrete lumps by hand, but ditched this idea in favour of making something more perfectly spherical. I needed some type of mould, and after much head scratching — and while cooking a stir fry — a wok sprang to mind. Perfectly suited! I found a really big one about 70 centimetres (about 30 inches) in diameter at a Chinese supermarket, plus a couple of regular-sized ones. We made up a dozen or so and lightened the weight of the concrete by using vermiculite in the mix. The moon rocks, as they have come to be known, are pure folly and the three that have been mosaiced provide funky little colour bursts through the garden.

Drawing inspiration from nature when making a garden doesn't mean that you have to slavishly re-create nature — a tall order in my book. Instead, like Lou and Anthony's garden, they can very much be human places, somewhere the garden maker can make his or her mark, while always using nature as a starting point.

BUILDING THE SCREENS

The screens were a constantly evolving element right from their inception. There are two screens: one curved and the other straight. The materials for the screens were first collected in varying widths and lengths and laid out on the ground to provide the full range of choice. With no definite plan the timber (Merbau hardwood) and fibre cement sheeting (painted pale grey) were attached first to the support posts, one piece at a time, while we constantly checked and monitored the overall composition. Over the base of timber and fibre cement sheeting, strips of hot pink and red Perspex, aluminium and mirrored stainless steel were added one piece at a time. Again, after each piece was added we checked the overall composition before moving onto the next piece.

The screen was originally inspired by the strips of bark that were shed by the surrounding eucalypts. The idea began as a screen made from woven bark and eventually evolved into the final adventurous result.

This is a garden that at first glance you would assume is a slice of natural coastal heath typical of the area. But as you move through it you start to realize that a design-aware hand has shaped this place. The gravel garden (right) is a study in scale, balance and proportion: tufts of native grasses such as *Stipa stipoides* are contrasted against shaped spheres of *Correa alba* (top far right) as well as the languid form of silver cushion bush (*Leucophyta brownii*). A billowing lawn of wallaby grass (*Danthonia* sp.) (centre far right) and a kangaroo paw (*Macropidia* sp.) (bottom far right) propagated by Jane.

A RESTORED BUSHLAND GARDEN

MAKING SENSE

DESIGNED BY JANE BURKE AND FIONA BROKHOFF

FROM A PLACE OF ART AND SCULPTURE INSPIRED BY NATURAL BUSH, TO AN ARTISTICALLY RESTORED SLICE OF BUSH; BOTH GARDENS WITH INVISIBLE BOUNDARIES

Jane Burke's garden is amazing. At the risk of sounding sycophantic I'd venture to say 'Offshore' is possibly one of Australia's best.

When Jane and her husband Peter bought the property in 1975 it was covered in a mass of tea tree (*Melaleuca alternifolia*). As it was adjacent to national park that comprised rugged heath, coastal bushland and sand dunes all a stone's throw from Bass Strait, Victoria, Jane assumed this tea tree 'forest' on their property had been there forever. Before long, however, Jane realized that due to past land clearing the tea tree had in fact invaded the area and had taken over as a monoculture.

With characteristic determination, Jane took on the task of revegetating the land to bring it back to its condition prior to European colonization — a process greatly assisted when she subsequently qualified as a botanist at Melbourne University in 1995.

At no point did Jane set out to 'design' a garden. It was more a case of solving functional issues like wind protection and an overriding aim to reinstate an ecosystem that was as close as possible to what would have originally been there. This, in essence, has been the garden's saving grace. The garden's evolution has been slow and considered. The feeling and integrity of the dune country has been maintained, helped in part by the complete lack of any perceivable boundaries or fencelines marking the edges of the property.

The most deliberate injection of design was introduced when Jane's friend, neighbour and garden designer, Fiona Brokhoff (who coincidentally is the owner and creator of another of Australia's great gardens, 'Karkalla', nextdoor) helped in the laying out of the gravel garden — the space which is now the 'heart' of the garden. Fiona was a great teacher of design principles such as scale, proportion and composition, and Jane was clearly a receptive pupil.

Now this is the bit that makes me all starstruck about this garden. A native vegetation regeneration project is one thing,

but to re-create or repair an ecosystem in a way that brings out the strong design aesthetic of the plants and materials you use to do that, is something else all together.

The gravel garden is where the magic happens. If you were blindfolded and led into this area, and the blindfold removed to reveal the scene, you could quite easily think you were in untouched dune and heath country. But then you'd realize that there was something more at play: a discerning eye has assessed the inherent design qualities of each plant, considered the palette of materials and put it all together so you're able to appreciate and celebrate the qualities — be they physical or atmospheric — that make this place unique.

Big fluffy tufts of *Stipa stipoides* are contrasted against shaped and rounded mounds of *Correa alba*, while the ghostly silver *Leucophyta brownii* comes close to stealing the show. Generous, broad, snaking paths of compacted shell grit and old timber pier beams casually dissect the garden while the odd beach find — an old craypot or perhaps a piece of cuttlefish — speaks quietly of where we are.

Beyond the visually stunning, and ecological, layers to this garden, Jane also uses it as both a plant laboratory and seed collection area, trialling different native species, mostly local to the area, for potential commercial horticulture markets and regeneration projects.

The wallaby grass (*Danthonia* species), in particular, has been an ongoing project. Exploring its potential as an alternative to more traditionally exotic lawn grasses, over a number of patient years Jane has been able to create a dense sward of grass, diligently weeding and coaxing it to grow into a 'lawn'. Sometimes green and fluffy, sometimes straw-coloured and hayfield like, the wallaby grass is important as a simple low-lying element that serves to balance the tufts of grass and heath of the gravel garden.

For me this garden is the ultimate physical manifestation of that phrase I hold dear — a sense of place. Using the soundest of ecological ideals and finely tuned aesthetics, Jane has created a garden that is a pure understated celebration of where it is. When you walk into it you get a very rich sense of where you are. It owes absolutely nothing to any borrowed concept of what a garden is, or is meant to be. As soon as I'd seen it, I knew that whenever I was struggling to get across this whole concept of creating stunning gardens that are totally in touch with where they are, all I'd have to do was hold up a photo of Jane's garden.

Overlooking the gravel garden towards the guest cottage that was once the only accommodation on the property (left). Using plants native to the area and setting them out in a natural fashion that is at once aesthetically satisfying and true to the way they would occur in natural heath, Jane has created a garden that has a richly developed sense of place. The stunning silver cushion bush (bottom right).

INDEX

Published in 2005 by Murdoch Books Pty Limited.

Murdoch Books Australia
Pier 8/9, 23 Hickson Road,
Millers Point NSW 2000
Phone: +61 (0)2 8220 2000; Fax: +61 (0)2 8220 2558

Murdoch Books UK Limited
Erico House, 6th Floor North, 93–99 Upper Richmond Road,
Putney, London SW15 2TG
Phone: +44 (0)20 8785 5995; Fax: +44 (0)20 8785 5985

Chief executive: Juliet Rogers
Publisher: Kay Scarlett
Design concept and design: Marylouise Brammer
Editor: Diana Hill
Design manager: Vivien Valk
Photographers: Michael Wee (all except where specified); Brendan Moar (front cover; and pages 4 main lavender image lower R; 14; 15; 24 far L; 33 top L; across 36–7; across 40–41; 42 far R; 44; 45; 48; 49; 50 far L; across 52–3; 54; across 54–55 top and bottom; 66–7 all shots within mood board; 82–3 all shots within mood board; across 88–9; across 90–1; 91 top R, upper R, bottom R; 98–9 all shots within mood board; 114–15 all shots within mood board; 128–9 all shots within mood board; 144–5 all shots within mood board; 158–9 all shots within mood board; 174–5 all shots within mood board)
Illustrations and garden plans: Brendan Moar
Photo management: Amanda McKittrick
Production: Monika Vidovic and Monika Paratore

National Library of Australia Cataloguing-in-Publication Data
Moar, Brendan. Grounded. Includes index. ISBN 1 74045 465 0. 1. Moar, Brendan.
2. Gardens – Design. 3. Landscape architecture. I. Title. 712. 6

Printed by Midas Printing (Asia) Ltd. PRINTED IN CHINA. First printed 2005.

Text © Brendan Moar and XYZnetworks Pty Limited 2005
Design © Murdoch Books Pty Limited 2005
Photography © XYZnetworks Pty Limited and Michael Wee 2005: page 4 (except main lavender image lower R); 5; across pages 10–11; 16 far L; 18 above; 19 far R; 20–1; across 22–3; across 24–25; 25 far R; 26 top L, top R; 27–31; across 32–3 top; 33 top R; across 34–5; 36 top L; 37 top R; 38–40; 43 top R; 46 top L; across 50–1; 52 top L; 53 top L, bottom L; 55 top R; 56–9; across 60–1; 61 top R; 62–5; 68; 7–5; 97; 101–7; 127; 131–7; 142–3; 147–151; 157; 161–7; 172–3; 177–83
Photography © Michael Wee 2005: back cover and pages 6; 12–13; across 16–17; across 18–19; 26 bottom; across 32–3 bottom; across 42–3; across 46–7; 47; 53 top R; 60 top L; 66–7 main mood board; 76–9; 81; 82–3 main mood board; 85–7; 91 lower R; 92–5; 98–9 main mood board; 108–11; 113; 114–15 main mood board; 117–25; 128–9 main mood board; 138–41; 144–5 main mood board; 152–5; 158–9 main mood board; 168–71; 174–5 main mood board; 184–8
Photography © Brendan Moar 2005: front cover and pages 4 main lavender image lower R; 14; 15; 24 far L; 33 top L; across 36–7; across 40–41; 42 far R; 44; 45; 48; 49; 50 far L; across 52–3; 54; across 54–55 top and bottom; 66–7 all shots within mood board; 82–3 all shots within mood board; across 88–9; across 90–1; 91 top R, upper R, bottom R; 98–9 all shots within mood board; 114–15 all shots within mood board; 128–9 all shots within mood board; 144–5 all shots within mood board; 158–9 all shots within mood board; 174–5 all shots within mood board

This book is published to accompany the television series *Moar Gardening* which is broadcast on The LifeStyle Channel, FOXTEL and AUSTAR.

Readers of this book must ensure that any work or project undertaken complies with local legislative and approval requirements relevant to their particular circumstances. Furthermore, this work is necessarily of a general nature and cannot be a substitute for appropriate professional advice.